CADENCE

St. Mark's Nature Refuge
Diane Reitz

CADENCE

Florida State Poets Association
Anthology Thirty-Nine ▪ 2021

Published by
the Florida State Poets Association
with book Design by CHB Media

Editors
Gary Broughman
JC Kato
Elaine Person

ISBN: 9798488544154

Printed in the United States of America

www.floridastatepoetsassociation.org

Cover Photographs
Front cover:
Sunset at Canaveral Seashore
Stan Sujka

Back cover:
At the Jetty
New Smyrna Dunes Park
Mark Andew James Terry

Acknowledgements

THIS THIRTY-NINTH ANNUAL EDITION of the Florida State Poets Association anthology is now the fifth to wear the name, *Cadence*. Perhaps this will be the last year we mention that little fact. The name *Cadence* is now entrenched. This year's volume of *Cadence* is published in a difficult time. *Cadence* is usually introduced as a highlight of FSPA's annual convention in October, but because of the pandemic the 2021 gathering was converted to virtual. Of course, Covid hasn't stopped poets from writing, and the quality of the poetry in this latest volume speaks to the health of the word-based arts in Florida. While whirlwinds swirl in the culture, poets are keeping the creative flame alive, and in so doing are proving that reconciliation remains possible if we will only think with the heart. Was there ever a time when loving kindness, compassion and acceptance were more needed?

Another annual feature of *Cadence* is publication of winners in the Florida Student Poetry contest for both middle and high school students. However, this year's contest was another casualty of the pandemic. We will back with our wonderful student poems in 2022.

This volume of *Cadence* also includes winning selections in twenty-six categories of FSPA's annual poetry awards contest, which is open to all poets, no matter where they practice their craft. The FSPA contest is managed by Marc Davidson, taking over from Mary Rogers-Grantham. Our thanks to Marc for another successful contest, and to Mary for all she did over the past years.

Finally, thanks to all the poets who submitted their work, to the chapter leaders who encouraged their members, and to my co-editors, Elaine Person and JC Kato.

— Gary Broughman, Editor

The Poems

St. Mark's Nature Refuge Diane Reitz. 2
The Edge of Land and Sea Juliana Romnes. 10

FSPA CHAPTERS AND THEIR POETS

Big Bend Poets
Linda Marie Cossa, Hot Stuff. 13
Gordon L. Magill, As I contemplate those famous poets 14

Citrus Poets
Joan Hoag Hitchcock, In Memory 16

Live Poets Society of Daytona Beach
Cherelyn Bush, Blue Springs 18
Llewellyn McKernan, I No Longer Want To Be 19
Ellen Nielsen, After the Plague Year 20
Bruce Woodworth, Carver of Warmth. 21

Miami Poets
Connie Goodman-Milone, Haiku 23
Tere Starr, Spider Weaves. 24

New River Poets
Suzanne S. Austin-Hill, Poetry, An Ointment for 454,209+ Families 26
John F. Foster, Florida's Curse 27
J.C. Kato, Ekphrastic Haiku 28
Gary Ketchum, Committing The Perfect Clime 29
Beverly A. Joyce, The Classical Poets Society. 31
Marisa Moks-Unger, Curtain Call 32
Susan Stahr, Daydreams 33
Cheryl A. Van Beek, Archaeology 34
Janet Watson, Giving Him the World 35
Betty Ann Whitney, The Glory of Trees. 36

North Florida Poetry Hub
Chris Kastle, Dancing Zebras. 38
Barrie Levine, What Makes a Great Coffee Shop? 39
Howard Moon, Bacon and Frybread 40
Sharon Scholl, Monday. 42
Ruth Van Alstine, Fo•ram•i•nif•e•ra. 43
Paula Veloso Babadi, Hands for Bread 44

Orlando Area Poets
Teresa TL Bruce, unRESOLVEd on New Year's Day. 47
Lela E. Buis, White Buffalo Maiden 48
Gary Childress, Satisfactory Complaint 49
Michele Cuomo, Crone Poem. 50
Chris Flocken, Sunlight Savior 51
Nikki Fragala Barnes, kiss good night 52
Alice R. Friedman, Finches 53
Peter M. Gordon, Pop 54
Carlton Johnson, The Order of Time 55

Ngan Ling Lung, Hong Kong. 56
Holly Mandelkern, The Blue Danube 57
Mary Marcelle, Later that afternoon. 58
Frank T Masi, A Happy Funeral 59
Diane Neff, Another Door. 61
Elaine Person, Urgent Care Recommendations. 62
Diane Reitz, Gone Too Soon.. 63
Rosa C. Rodriguez, The Hug of Time.. 64
Lynn Schiffhorst, I Feel For The Devil 65
Carolynn Scully, Courage.. 66
Lyn Sedwick, Ars Poetica. 67
Juli Simon, Hurricane Season.. 68
Shelley Stocksdale, Birds Roost 69
Emily Sujka, Overcomplicated 70
Dr. Jenni Sujka, 10 Years From Now 71
Stan K. Sujka, Memories.. 72
Mark Andrew James Terry, For Sister Twinkle 73
Cheryl Lynn West, Lyman Lee Home 74
Shari Yudenfreund-Sujka, The Peach 76

Poetry for the Love of It
Laurence Amuso, De Naturibus 78
Sue Hansen, Sorta Rap. 79
Louise Pare-Lobinske, on mom's first heavenly birthday. 80
Linda Whitefeather, "Good-bye" 82

Space Coast Poets
Nancy K. Hauptle MacInnis, This American Has A Dream 84
Anne-Marie Simonton, Ritual. 85

Sunshine Poets
Angie M. Mayo, The Stranger in the Mirror 87
Cheri Neuman Herald, Lessons From Lockdown 88

Tomoka Poets
B.J. Alligood, My Constellation 90
Gary Broughman, Watering Weeds 91
Niki Byram, Surfer Jack and The Enchanted Forest. 92
Mitzi J. Coats, Refugees 93
Sonja Jean Craig, Seed Song 95
Marc Davidson, Snare Drum Weather.. 96
Linda Eve Diamond, Unwritten 98
Mary-Ann Westbrook, What And Where 99
Brown Pelican at Rest, New Smyrna Beach, Daniel L. Stone. .. .. .100

MEMBERS AT LARGE
JG Annino, Lucky 102
Swati Bagga, Life .. .. .103
Pat Bastendorf, Mixed Cinquain .. .. .105
Hanh Chau, Dew Drop .. .. .106
Christine Cock, Ode to the Paddle Fan .. .. .107
Barry A. Dimick, A Summer Night 108
Melody Dean Dimick, Marianna Reform School 109

Ann Favreau, The Glassblower 110
Raymond Fones, Afterwards 111
Charles Hazelip, What Makes a Friend a Friend? 112
Nina Heiser, Orange Juice 113
Dr. Emory D. Jones, Deep Freeze. .114
Judith Krum, The Line Between 115
Cheryl Licata, Untimely Unity 116
Mary Ellen Orvis, On the Beach in Northern Ireland. 117
Dennis Rhodes, Stopping by the Sea on a Rainy Evening 118
Al Rocheleau, On Vengeance.. 119
Mary Rogers-Grantham, An Argument in Rhythm 120
Evelyn Ann Romano, *La Mer*.. 121
Juliana Romnes, The Calm Before. .122
Tim Schulz, Heart Strings 123
Daniel L. Stone, Summer's Almost Gone 125
Daniel R. Tardona, Life in a Cardboard Box 126
Tanya R. Whitney, A Single Red Rose 127
Lady Liberty Replica, Orlando, Elaine Person. 128

FSPA CHANCELLORS
Silvia Curbelo, The Road Back 130
Denise Duhamel, From Here To Eternity 131
Carol Frost, How Music Came Into The City 132
Lola Haskins, Dominion.. 133
David Kirby, Man Catches Baby 134
Peter Meinke, An Old Soldier Soughing in the Dark 136
Virgil Suárez, Vibrational Reciprocity 137
Ibis Committee, Sonja Jean Craig.. .138

FSPA 2021 POETRY CONTEST WINNERS
Category 1 — FSPA Free Verse Award
Mary Rogers-Grantham, One Hundred and Thirty-Six 140
Category 2 — FSPA Formal Verse Award
Holly Mandelkern, Donne's Time and Our Time 141
Category 3 — The Live Poets Society Award
Stephen Stokes, Dry Run 142
Category 4 — Tomoka Poets Award
Marc Davidson, Ecclesia In Litore .143
Category 5 — Willard B. Foster Memorial Award
Sara Gipson, Soup Kitchen 144
Category 6 — The Rondeau Award
Joyce Shiver, Mother's Motto.. 145
Category 7 — June Owens Memorial Award
Robyn Weinbaum, Chris Dance. 146
Category 8 — The Poet's Vision Award
Joanne Vandegrift, The Reverend Sandhill Crane. 147
Category 9 — New River Poets Award
Beverly Smith-Tillery, Broken Promises 148

Category 10 — The Alfred Von Brokoph Award
Stephen Stokes, Your Body's Footprint 149
Category 11 — The Howard and Sandy Gordon Memorial Award
Diane Neff, Mothering 150
Category 12 — The Janet Brinkley Erwin Memorial Award
Shutta Crum, The Cat And I Look For Poems . . .. .152
Category 13 — The Noah Webster Award
Catherine Moran, Looking at the memorabilia 153
Category 14 — Kate Kennedy Memorial Award
Steven Leitch, I Hate Chocolate 155
Category 15 — Henrietta & Mark Kroah Founders Award
Carolynn J. Scully, Daddy-Daughter Dance 156
Category 16 — The Past President's Award
Jerri Hardesty, Oh By the Way, Which One's "Pink" 157
Category 17 — The Current Issues Award
COL (Ret) Beverly Smith-Tillery, The End of War in Afghanistan 158
Category 18 — The Orlando Area Poets Award
Cheryl A. Van Beek, Backdraft 159
Category 19 — Leslie Halpern Award
Mardi Knudsen, Magic Story for Falling Asleep 160
Category 20 — The Humor Award
Peter M. Gordon, CAT Scan Report 161
Category 21 — The Dorsimera Award
Barbara Blanks, Spring Jubilation 162
Category 22 — The Childhood Award
Carolynn J. Scully, Little Adventures. 163
Category 23 — The Weinbaum/Glidden Award
Michele Cuomo, Islip 164
Category 24 — The Enchantment Award
Cheryl A. Van Beek, Wing Beats 165
Category 25 — The Miami Poets Award
Mark Andrew James Terry, At a Friend's Grave 166
Category 26 — The Ekphrastic Poem Award
Mark Andrew James Terry, Those I Never Knew 167

Playalinda Beach, Cheri Neuman Herald. 168

About the Florida State Poets Association.. 169
History, Objectives, Association with the National Federation. 170

Paddleboarding, Daytona Beach, Daniel L. Stone 171

The Edge of Land and Sea
Juliana Romnes

FSPA
CHAPTER POETS

BIG BEND POETS

Linda Marie Cossa

Hot Stuff

I am
a mystical mover and shaker
universal fixer
force of attraction holding
everything together just right
and I can actually bend light
the gravity of love
I am
all around you
even the air you breathe is me
from beginning creation I am
living forever I will always be
the atom of love
I am
surrounding you vibrating
no matter where you go
always with you there
I am everywhere
the sound of love
I am
what I am not, a riddle
a blank space without matter
dismissing friction so light travels
in the nothingness of everything
the vacuum of love
I am
hot stuff burning
with desire to get things done
my get up and go enables
the brain to think and plants to grow
from the sun afar
I am at one
with everything
under that star
the energy of love

Gordon L. Magill

As I contemplate those famous poets

As I contemplate those famous poets
our age remembers, and perhaps the next,
how they came to their recognition and success
I wonder what the formula, the recipe
the physics of profundity or sheer simplicity
what alchemy of brain, and wit, and luck?

A envious voice within me snorts: "it's simple really…
give me a thousand poets, and a few, like cream
will rise thick and buttery to the top."

But then a chorus of far off voices I hear
of all the unknown poets in the world
who lived their lives, dreamed their dreams,
wrote verses between jobs and before dawn
never gave a damn to win a contest or prize,
fell in love, married, divorced, found success or ruin,
eventually grew old, faded into that good night

Were glad if heard by only a few
especially fellow poets and friends
who listened with open hearts and empathic mind

Or were doubly glad if
they reached the hearts of the sad,
the beaten, those balanced on the edge,
and of children, also the very aged:
any and all who needed to hear their words

That made the difference; it wasn't the fame
public notice, the publicity, academic acclaim
but the change in a face, a smile, or a laugh −
the nod of agreement that bridges the gap
between strangers:
poems of words won of living deeply
shared freely with no need of applause.

CITRUS CHAPTER

Joan Hoag Hitchcock

In Memory
(Villanelle)

Mom died peacefully two years ago today,
Transitioning to a spiritual plane,
Passing into a space beyond her earthly stay.

Transcending toward a sublime love, I pray,
A place of calming peace with no need for pain,
Mom died peacefully two years ago today.

Either a short visit or extended play,
To somewhere with no dependence on a cane,
Passing to a space beyond her earthly stay.

A spirit realm where time's not measured by day,
Nor are there any seasons that wax and wane,
Mom died peacefully two years ago today.

On to a heaven space that guides each new stray,
Toward a brilliant light far from any rain,
Passing to a space beyond her earthly stay.

Through mysterious changes so far away,
Which enlighten the spirit with each new gain,
Mom died peacefully two years ago today,
Passing to a space beyond her earthly stay.

LIVE POETS
OF DAYTONA BEACH

Cherelyn Bush

Blue Springs

The only location to see a manatee
The water temperature is 72 degrees
The paths are grass and dirt
The interior color is a golden hue
The spring jet generates tons of water
The opening is cavernous
The park allows swimming
The swimmers ruin the ecosystem
See it now

Llewellyn McKernan

I No Longer Want To Be

a nymph
locked inside the branches
of a tree. Not even the royal
hollow oak where
King Charles once hid
from all his enemies
is spacious
enough for me.

I don't
want my hands to be leaves
fluttering with
the breeze, nor do I want my topmost
outpost one
to stupidly gaze
at the sky all day long,
and never look
down to see what's happening
on the ground below,
where what takes place
is all of earth's worthwhile
activities.

My roots
are my feet, and they were made
for walking, for taking
a path here, one
there that veers off
the path so
that at last I can see
the flower of the hour that
the Maker of Trees
made for me.

Ellen Nielsen

After the Plague Year

like birth, it's a mix of joy and pain
we squeeze out of our
singular tunnels
bruised lives
misshapen
after a
year of
isolation
tender skin flecked
with blood and mucous
breathing deep expanding our lungs
rusty voices bawling out our new songs

Bruce Woodworth

Carver of Warmth

He's up at first light, sometimes before
with a file and a stone and his chisels and more.
Gotta keep 'em keen if you wanna stay in the hunt.
No work gets done with an edge that's blunt.

In the middle of the floor on a sturdy stand
sits the lone wood block waiting to feel his hand.
But first comes study, and the knowing of the grain.
No chips will fly till he forms a plan.

There's knots and bark and the lovely burl
and grain that tightens and runs in swirls.
There's a hidden figure in this core of wood
you can almost see it if you know how to look.

With his mind made up and his mallet poised
that favorite chisel is soon employed
and the chips will fly and the wood reveal
its secrets hidden for a hundred year.

The hours fly by and she calls for a rest
the work not done but it's for the best.
His back is screaming and his shoulders ache.
Even the artist needs to take a break.

And when he comes back, there'll be study again
for the block's still revealing its soul within.
its heart, its life, it offers up
To the hand of the man, once the wood is struck.

And when at last no more chips fall
the work is done, three weeks in all
he rests those hands on his cramping thighs
and feels the glow of a dream realized.

This one'll look nice on the side of the hearth
until winter's depth seals its fate, come March.
Then the wood will pop and the sparks will fly
and they'll toast its warmth with a last goodbye.

MIAMI POETS

Connie Goodman-Milone

Iridescent blue
hummingbird sips sweet water
at turn of twilight

Tere Starr

Spider Weaves

And when eyes meet far off, our sense is such
That, spider-like, we feel the tenderest touch.
— John Dryden

Spider weaves her web of words
to lure like spirits,
call them home.
Now you and I, while
entertaining new realities,
adventures, are giving gifts of
spontaneity, of joy
to our souls.

Did your web or mine do the catching?
Are our webs illusions,
translucent, intertwined?
Will we transcend their boundaries,
add dimensions to our minds?

Will we survive extended moments,
restrictions of time and place,
live in the real world,
limitations of pain and space?
Words, more words and webs are built.
Fantasies' sweet music soothes.
Words leave a sparkling trace.

So spider, keep the words up,
weave your web of stars.
Spider, gather what you need,
for every spirit that you touch,
your light in turn will seed
eternal timeless spaces,
stars of hope,
worlds of love,
in heaven's darkest places.

NEW RIVER POETS

Suzanne S. Austin-Hill

Poetry, An Ointment for 454,209+ Families

At the break of dawn ... alone in the sounds of your breathing

The day's chorales go unsung because one voice is missing.
Orchestrations remain unheard because one seat is empty.

Same as yesterday daylight shines on the absence.

This dissonant chord will never resolve;

can't begin to describe
   the sickness whose only cure
   is to ask the angels
   to loan your loved one to you.

The silence is yours to deal with.

A single, shimmering sun beam will guide you ...
      alone in the sounds of your breathing.

John F. Foster

Florida's Curse

In the wake of weighty rain,
land succumbs to tortured strain.

Sandy loam engorged, a sponge,
owes to gravity its plunge

into yawning cavities,
taking houses, roads and trees.

Deep depression settles in,
denting earth's now fragile skin.

Downward heaving rubble slips
into pit's apocalypse.

Gaping hole, a canker sore,
e'er metastasizing more.

Where the curse may next attack
from below, we cannot track.

Sink holes seem to lie in wait.
Shadows in the Sunshine State.

J.C. Kato

Ekphrastic Haiku

harsh winds east and west
buries mounds of silenced pleas
our mountain listens

Estelle Ishigo
Heart Mountain Japanese Internment Camp, Wyoming, 1942

Gary Ketchum

Committing The Perfect Clime

Twain—Mark, not Shania—was said to have said,
"Everybody talks about the weather but
nobody does anything about it."
Well, our mobile society means we can do
something about it—MOVE—but where?

Hmm … how 'bout Eastern Seaboard?
Sensational summers, awesome autumns
capes, beaches, boardwalks
but ooh, the Noreasters, perfect storms, wicked winters!
Aye-uh. Thumbs down on Down East.

Upper Midwest: Great Lakes, great little lakes as well
for fishing, boating, swimming.
Whoa, there! There's woe there, too!
Terrifying tornadoes to ravage us or whiteout blizzards
destined to freeze our gizzards.
Twain—Shania, not Mark—sang,
"That don't impress me much."

Consider West Coast mild winters north
Mediterranean winters south but
beware *El Niño* and *La Niña,*
monsoons and mudslides.
Twain—Mark, not Shania—once remarked,
"The coldest winter I ever spent
was summer in San Francisco!"

Well, at least there's the sunny Southeast,
sub-tropical with wonderfully warm winters,
though, summer's humid heat's a beast
AND y'all have hurricanes, him-i-canes
haunting and daunting.

America's weather ain't leadin'
to any guaranteed Eden.
Whither I go, whether I go,
weather will bewilder me so
I either stay home or pick
my particular imperfect paradise.

Beverly A. Joyce

The Classical Poets Society

If all the poets from the ages
From our textbook pages
Could get together for a reading,
That would be one grand meeting.
Henry Longfellow could be the host
Telling of George Washington's ghost.
Emily Dickinson could bring her cake
For William Shakespeare and William Blake.
While in hand a cup and saucer,
We would listen to Geoffrey Chaucer.
Percy Bysshe Shelley would be there
Sir Walter Raleigh and Walter de la Mare,
And the gathering would be incomplete
Without Robert Frost and John Keats.
Poems from James Whitcomb Riley
Mary Oliver and Elinor Wylie.
Attending would be Edgar Allan Poe
Walt Whitman and Philip Freneau.
It would be quite a bash
With e.e. cummings and Ogden Nash,
Robert W. Service and Bret Harte.
This list is just the very start.
As our reading continued on,
We'd enjoy John Donne.
Way too many to name here,
But I have named a few.
Oh, yes, I must not forget
You're definitely invited, too.
If all the poets could unite,
It would be a poetic delight.

Marisa Moks-Unger

Curtain Call

Problem-free as a toddler
stepping on the stage of my life.
Tippy-toed with supporting cast,
stepping on the stage of my life
"The perfect only child," Mom said then.
Stepping on the stage of my life.

Suddenly – swish, the curtain closed.
Just then my rolling credits froze.
Rock-a-bye-babies birthed their woes.
More loss, more tears. Nobody knows.
Exit stage left. Off-script for years.
Pantomime to placate Dad's fears.

Realizing, I shouldered the loss.
Stepping on the stage of my life.
Script in hand, options are so vast -
stepping on the stage of my life.
Firm-footed now, the footlights call.
Stepping on the stage of my life.

Susan Stahr

Daydreams

On this cool shady hill under broad outstretched branches
I dare here to dream and think of my chances
Of being whomever I wish – and to bring it about
It's my secret place to sit – to dance – to shout

In my private time alone here I hold all the powers
Doing whatever I wish for hours and hours
I can rule vast new kingdoms I've never before known
Or just sit and ponder on a grand ivory throne

Create brave new worlds as my thoughts take me away
Have a prince win my hand as the dragons he'll slay
Then at the nod of my head or the kiss of a breeze
I'm a great ship's captain on the black raging seas

In the blink of an eye I can travel so far
Launch into space and speed through the stars
I can scale every mountain - climb all the trees
Be covered by diamonds and skate on the breeze

I could stay here forever – just sit and think
Realize my every wish – just through a blink
I'd never get tired of the people I'd meet
But it'll all have to wait now – 'cause it's time to EAT!

Cheryl A. Van Beek

Archaeology

The present discovers the past
in the house's breath, its bones, its bedrock.
Time-sharpened, toothy thoughts chew through wood.
Kindness resprouts in broken cement.

The lock sticks with a crust of rusted plans.
The oak floor holds music in its knotty grain—
their humming, whistling, dancing.
Stairs sigh and creak with tiptoeing secrets.

In the attic, hardened relics of indecision roll
back and forth like rolly-polly pill bugs curled into balls.
In the mosaic of cracked tile, blame
rots under a fault-line of misunderstanding.

Old friends—lilacs and jonquils still sleep in the garden,
reawakening each season to break ground.
Like ashes of scrapped passions, skin cells
crumble into the yard with spent stucco.

Air pockets sewn by ambitious ants
are lined with loamy scents of hope
that rise to open the house and free the land.

Faceting through time—even the crush of regret,
vibrations of their tender embraces, laughter,
the stinging salt of wasted worry,
the hot, magnetic pull of fingers entwined—all join

to form crystals in the earth like Herkimer diamonds.
The present brushes off the dirt,
shining light through the prisms of memory—
sharp, blurred, in ever-shifting sparkle.

"Reprinted with the permission of *Odet,* Chapter Two Press, and the author."

Janet Watson

Giving Him the World

His child-hands spun
the large sphere in its mahogany stand.
Watching the Earth whirl
at one's command is heady stuff,
and such power lures
whether we are innocent or mighty.
The library's globe
gave me the opportunity
to tell a five-year-old
the story of the world.

I presented to him
the vast blue of oceans and invited him
to climb mountain ranges
with his small fingers.
He slid them across broad continents,
and where he traced borders
of multi-colored nations,
no battles raged.
He discovered poles and parallels.
His eyes traveled the equator,
which floated invisibly on the sea,
when many years later
he sailed over it.

Recently I found an old globe
much like that library one.
It will be a new gift for him,
and I think he will like it,
although it turns stiffly on its axis
in a battle-weary stand
and its faded surface shows shrinkage.
Illuminated, the sphere spills light,
for this miniature world appears
to be coming apart at the seams--
so like the real one, which I,
regrettably, must leave to my son.

Betty Ann Whitney

The Glory of Trees

> In loving remembrance
> of June Owens

Someday we may sit again
under a tree, as we did
at the New River Library
for an afternoon of poetry.

In the whole range of varieties
in our poet-tree-circle, you
were the nourishment,
a fine dense tree stretching skyward,
like the *wind-caught hemlock* likened
in your poetry, spreading your span
of life into volumes, comforting,
not only your circle, but valuable to all.

Your hope, your love for us awakened
in us to an aim to grow great and handsome,
gracefully green, with hardy branches,
which, when broken off from the main,
became deeply lobed and recognized
among the better-known, erect in form,
suitable to grow huge forests of our own.

Perhaps from the beginning
you were blessed to pass quickly,
to be pieced together again by angels . . .

without end,
under a moon, full enough
for you to see the open doors of your house,
built in the sharp of rocks and hard
of mountains where you may *sleep*
gratefully under those tree-line
trembling stars
twinkled from your pen.

36

NORTH FLORIDA POETRY HUB

Chris Kastle

Dancing Zebras

Equine species white on black
Stately stripes upon your back
Chocolate swirls in clotted cream
Circling smooth from grass to stream

Butterflies by ones and twos
Pick your partner time to choose
Floating, fluttering yellow on black
Shapely stripes upon your back

Tiny minnow swimming strong
Racing currents speed along
Silky stripes along your back
Glinting flash of silvery black

Zebras dancing cheek to cheek
Every nuance tres unique

Barrie Levine

What Makes A Great Coffee Shop?

First, it helps to be in Rome
standing at a marble counter
with fresh brewed expresso,
a framed black and white
of Sophia Loren
staring at you
to add a voluptuous note

Perhaps the Neue Gallery
on 86th and Fifth
fashioned precisely
after a Viennese coffeehouse,
your cup and saucer
set on pressed linen
accompanied by a tray of tarts
and other small confections,
not quite ready to drink or eat
until divinely paired

Or maybe Paris in the fall,
walking through the Louvre
until fatigue by portrait
and landscape confounds you . . .
then, on to Angeline's
for refreshment,
the waiter setting
a chilled bottle of Perrier
at the corner table
reserved for you
and your ardent lover

Howard Moon

Bacon and Frybread

Sizzling bacon
Brings back memories
Of Sunday morning breakfasts
Family gathered around a worn Formica table
Sunday was "leaf day"
The table leaf retrieved from
Its hiding place under the bed
Extra chairs from around the house
The expanded table would seat eight comfortably
With extended family
We always managed seating for ten or more adults
The children eating on the porch
Mom and the aunts in the kitchen cooking
Grandmother on a stool
Supervising with her experienced eye
"Watch that bacon – crispy not burned"
"Biscuits smell done"
"That grease is ready for frybread"
Men sitting on the dilapidated porch
Exchanging what euphemistically passed for "news"
Us children scattered about
Just not underfoot in the kitchen
Sunday's sounds and smells were special
Part of growing up on the Reservation
Good memories
The best
I am shaken from my waking dream
By the waitress
"Here's your coffee"
"Having your regular this morning?"
"Order up"
The bacon continues to sizzle
Smells pour from the kitchen
My new Sunday morning
Miles from the Reservation
No longer the poor Indian boy just getting by
Now a successful businessman

Degrees on the wall
Sundays I miss the Rez as we use to call it
Family crowding around the table
I miss the community that poverty forced on us
Neighbors half-a-mile away were still – close
In white suburbia I over-look my neighbors' living room
I barely know their name
And would never call them close
I long for the lifestyle I struggled so hard to escape
This life my parents worked extra jobs for me to have
The advantages bought by my mother's long hours
At the loom making authentic Injun rugs
My brothers sisters and I are scattered to the four winds
All living better lives – or so we believe

But on Sunday mornings sometimes I long
For frybread dipped in bacon grease that would
run down the front of my shirt

Sharon Scholl

Monday

and we all begin again –
the failed suicide
the newly sober drunk
restart their lethal quest.

The terminally ill whose first thought
on opening an eye must be
Oh Damn!

the student whose study in wee hours
faces the exposure of a critical exam

the traveling sales rep whose exhausted sleep
erased all clues to where his body landed

the migrant whose first thought must be
translated to some foreign language

the new parent who hears a wailing cry
and suddenly recalls it's not the cat

They and all the rest of us collect
our weary bones, our shattered expectations,
and start the morning chores
that put life back together.

Ruth Van Alstine

Fo•ram•i•nif•e•ra

Lowly, yet ages enduring,
nature's single cell creatures,
stewards of a planet's history,
nature's catalyst, metaphoric beauties.

Stand as witness Bahama's Harbour,
arise pink forams protist planktons,
afloat in ocean currents and estuaries,
to weave, sift amidst soft coral sands,
ardent lovers entwine, embrace,
encompass the warm cerulean seas,
emerge as peach-kissed beaches,
from humble foraminifera cells.

Paula Veloso Babadi

Hands for Bread

(Dastah baraye Nun)
In memory of my Persian sister-in-law Goltala Jafari Babadi

"Don't learn to make bread," her mother said.
"It's hard work, your hands will grow heavy as
lead."
"I want to be like you, I love to help you
give bread."
"I'll teach you."
She was twelve.

"Study hard in America," she said
biting her lip as her eldest son carried
one small suitcase
packed with his uncle's favorite thin bread
and two changes of clothing.
She was twenty-eight.

"The Iraqi bombers are here, let's go!" her children cried.
"But we need our flour and water jugs,
what will you eat?"
"Naneh, everyone else is running to the mountainside!"
"Hide in the drainage pipes, I'm coming right behind you."
She fed her eight children and neighbors in
clay caves
with "nun lavash" crafted by hands and arms
strengthened through years of practice.
She was thirty-seven.

"Ammeh Goltala, can we try?"
"You watch me." She sat cross-legged on our kitchen floor,
my grandsons peering across the massive basin,
studying her knead to perfection with
rock-hard arms.
In the light of Florida dawn, outside waiting for her,
the gas fire-ring heated inside our homemade
metal cylinder.

Her fingers hurt shaping countless rows of round loaves
to flatten and toss and bake.
She still had hands for bread.
She was fifty- eight.

No one uses our rusted tin bread oven anymore.
She returned to her homeland -
streaked gray hair depicting years
of a body wracked with aches and pains.
Her second eldest son buys bread
at the market, these days -
the rise of her yeast deflated
by tired kidneys.
She was sixty-three.

My husband makes bread now.
It's not the same as his sister's.
I tried to mix and knead the dough,
make perfect round balls
to toss and cook.
But my hands weren't made for bread,
not like hers.
I miss her most when morning light slants
on the porch
where her hands used to toil for us.
She's gone,
and now forever grows in hearts
proofed with her love.
She will eternally have hands for bread.
She was seventy-three.

ORLANDO AREA POETS

Teresa TL Bruce

unRESOLVEd on New Year's Day

I won't cry over spilled
tabbouleh salad—slipped, spread across
kitchen tile from splattered fridge,
though drippy, oily pungent splashes
evoke specks of bile smeared and scattered.

Instead, I'll smile, faking myself into
making this inconvenient matter provoke
laughter. Cleanup cultivates mulling,
invokes chuckled puns, muttered quips.

From other room, grown daughter hollers,
"What's so funny?"

I grin, poke head around door.
"My writer's brain's inspired,
feeding on tabbouleh words."

Daughter swivels head, rolls eyes,
but she won't cry over spilled
Mom's sense. Instead, mouthy babe
sighs—then smirks. "Tabbouleh, huh?
No, Mom, it's quinoa."

Lela E. Buis

White Buffalo Maiden

Starvation stalks the plain.
Winter cold, the people move their tipis south,
Seeking after sustenance
for body and soul.

The specter follows, skeletal fingers
stroking the faces of babes in arms,
while mothers fold the blankets tight,
hoping to quiet the crying.

The scouts go out but find no herds.
Tied to mesquite and cottonwood,
red prayer ties flutter, forlorn,
calling for help in the wind.

"Come to us, O Ptesáŋwiŋ!"
And finally she comes, holy vision,
To bring us what we need.
The people rejoice!

Gary Childress

Satisfactory Complaint

Things could be worse
Or they could be better
But whenever
I think about it
I think first
Of what could be worse

If things were better
I could not complain
So then again
I'd not be happy
Just the same

For if I could not complain
Then that of which
I could not do
Would just as soon
Bother me too

Therefore
If I am asked
How am I
It seems to me
I ought to reply
That things are worse
But I am fine

Michele Cuomo

Crone Poem

The crone from around the corner
trots down the street with a cut-glass commemorative bowl
filled to overflowing with parrot food, the ibises like ladies-in-waiting
walking behind her, bowing as each seed drops.
She is going to the pond, of course. The neighbors shake their heads
and go back to watching the game on TV. They were sad for her
when her husband passed, but they did not know her well enough to visit.
And hasn't she changed since then?
Her hair in knots, her clothes strange
Her face dry, her eyes wet.
She had received the bowl for some achievement that has no meaning.
She raises it slightly as she comes upon the pond.
The Great Blue Heron is here—she knew it was a special occasion.
Honored that he makes an appearance. He is more important
than the Rosacea Duckbill, a pond celebrity, who always makes a splash,
or even the wizened wood stork, whom she knows and loves best.
Red, the Muscovy Duck, who came back after a year,
fat and friendly as ever,
is the first to notice she comes bearing gifts and is followed by his harem.
Muscovy Ducks hiss by way of greeting and are often misunderstood.
The Little Blue Heron is here, but quiet, as he knows there is no greatness
in his name.
As she rounds the pond, she looks for her Snake, coiled in an infinity sign
so they can stare at each other. But She is not here.
Finally, she finds a little knoll to place the bowl
and leaves it so that some traveler from the north
may drink pure rain water.
A slight smile before she steps onto the pavement
and starts back to the neighborhood.
She looks at the cement squares and wonders why
Humans love squares and God loves roundness.
The Muscovy Ducks hiss good-bye.

Chris Flocken

Sunlight Savior

As I sit by the window,
looking inward at the
unhappiness of my heart,
the sun finds me. It warms
my face. It dries my tears.
It soothes the ragged edges
of my soul.

I take a deep, cleansing breath.
I know I can go on.

Nikki Fragala Barnes

kiss good night

seven minutes, maybe eight — a time contained in lines, newspaper ink,
not memory, turns out safety is the equivalent of childhood monsters and
adolescent myths, an urban legend — I continue the deception with my
own children, like Santa Claus, like bedtime prayers, like the "content of
their character," and I lie, I lie, I lie, to make them feel safe I lie, my hands
smoothing their hair, and I can hear their phones (always) interrupting —
and I lie shushing and soothing, nine years to the day that Trayvon didn't
eat those skittles or feel that bedtime kiss blessing on his forehead, and I
lie for three more minutes, five more years, until they see their nakedness,
recognize the handwriting on the gift tags, know in their bones that I
cannot protect them, never could, that they were never protected

it was all a lie

maybe thirty more seconds

Alice R. Friedman

Finches

After Frannie left there
was no one to look after us
    my sister and me.

We were dropped off at the
Lisses' at Louse Point on the bay
Where Millie would cook and
We could play with Josie
    my sister and me.

We dressed in costumes
played records and
danced under the
watchfull eyes of
the finches whose quiet
quik, quik, soothed us

having been deserted
    by Frannie
    by parents

we danced away our sorrows
    my sister and me

watched by finches
trapped in a large cage
with the Lisses' at
Louse Point on the bay.

Peter M. Gordon

Pop

Manhattan Happy Hour, bar swamped by a sea
of tipsy thirty-somethings. I swim through
the crowd, wave to the blonde barkeep, who says,
"I'll be with you in a minute, Pop."

The universe whirled around me. *Pop.*
I'm not old; I'm young, but with physical challenges. *Pop.*
So what if the hairs I have left are grey and I wear bifocals? *Pop.*
I work out at a gym three times a week, a *half hour* each time. *Pop.*
I weigh a mere twenty-nine pounds more than I did in college. *Pop.*
Well, thirty-two pounds to be exact but I'm working on losing ten. *Pop.*
I'm married to a younger woman — *thirteen whole months* younger. *Pop.*
I watch the girls, glowing from their first cosmopolitans. *Pop.*
They lean toward the boys, who smile with perfect teeth. *Pop.*

No girls look at me.

Pop! I wonder, was the bartender right?
Pop! the balloon of my youth floats to the ceiling.
Pop! I see my father, stuck in bed in his nursing home.
Pop! I'm back in the bar, sipping single malt Scotch, neat.
Pop! My wrinkled reflection in the bar mirror winks at me.
Pop! Paddle through the crowd to the street stream of people.
Pop! I remember all my regrets, and stop, a rock in the river.
Pop! Fat man in a navy pea coat bumps me from behind, snarls,
      "*Whydontchakeep going!*"
Pop! Sounds like a good solution. I start moving.

Carlton Johnson

The Order of Time

This morning, outside my window,
on the green ground below,
a squirrel scavenges for food
completely unaware
of time, except perhaps that
there is a sun, a day, a nighttime,
but no calendar, no schedule, no
day-to-day planning. Now he's sniffing
the air, scanning the horizon for a furry
love mate—unaware of climate change,
plastics in the ocean, or the pandemic.

There is no order in the chaos
out-of-doors and yet

there is this squirrel
amongst the verdant grasses
just living life.

Ngan Ling Lung

Hong Kong

You are gone, taken away from me.
I have believed that you would always be there,
Awaiting my return,
Embracing your prodigal son.

Sorrow enters my body,
Joy leaking out of it.
My blood is saddened.
My taste is bitter.

You are caged, freedom deprived.
Words open a window to your soul,
Yet path your way to the jail.
Silence is violence.

Tears flow from my heart.
Rage bursts within.
My bones are shaking,
My teeth clench.

Safe here I am, you are not there.
It pains me to see your struggles,
Combating a fatal blow,
A bloody collapse.

Is it true, so true?
David is fighting Goliath.
An impossible battle to behold.
A courageous story unfolds.

I am always your child.
My pride rooted in you.
You are my love,
My beautiful home, my soul.

Holly Mandelkern

The Blue Danube

As Johann Strauss revived the mood
of Viennese when losses brewed,
he waltzed them to a river's waves,
a three-count-dance between the staves,
an homage to the Blue Danube.

He knew the water's turning hues,
her graying tints or reddish rouge.
By day it peaked and shimmered white,
jet black or silvered in the night,
but never wearing midnight blue...

When World War ends with Arrows Crossed
in crimson killings, bodies tossed.
The river bends to warn the Jews
(and saviors numbered just a few).
Even the Danube knows what's lost.

While touring scenic Budapest,
I sense a silent, drowned protest.
Cast iron shoes now mark their stance.*
What do we call this macabre dance?
Even a river now feels blue.

*The Shoes on the Danube Bank, a memorial conceived by
 Can Togay, erected on April 16, 2005, in Budapest, Hungary.

Mary Marcelle

Later that afternoon

Take that:
cards slammed on the table
with attitude, rage, flair or apprehension

Animated animosity in a game face
shows what we want to show and
hides
the rest.

I will calculate your strategy.
I will scheme to destroy your plans.
Danger awaits your every move.

The next hand is mine.

Frank T Masi

A Happy Funeral

Attending a funeral
is glum to some.
But death of trite words
makes a requiem fun.

I don't mind confessing
I'm an assassin for hire
preying on words
which stoke my ire.

I stalk the vernacular
with murderous intent
seeking to remove them
from sentences they rent.

Amazing should die,
torn from the tongue.
It's too much for too little
when words fail the young.

Weird deserves brutal death
placed in a word casket.
It scares nary a soul,
yet the sound tries to mask it.

Awesome needs a deep burial
killed by the masses.
It makes the simple *exceptional*
like using magnifying glasses.

Totally should be hung
viewed by a cheering crowd.
It compacts *eternal* into a ball
reducing a monster into a shroud.

Are there no word morgues,
places for dead phrases
killed in a duel
with an author's erasers?

It's a *happy funeral*
the day I can say,
"I buried the offenders
this wonderful day."

Diane Neff

Another Door

With rusty hinges, dusty floor,
The house showed true domestic war.
The chairs were broken, shelves unused,
Old wax dripped downward, candles fused

To wood and tile and even wall
And Callie thought she'd seen it all.
But voices wafted from the back
To lure her in the neighbor's shack,

Where in the narrow hall she walked
Through webs of spiders, dry as chalk
From years neglected, years untouched
By human hands or demon's clutch.

Then Callie saw a light ahead.
She stepped into its beam with dread
Another door was open wide
And as she entered, gasped and cried.

But still, the mystery's unsolved
Of who and why and what involved
Her as the target of this scheme?
A nightmare? Too high self-esteem?

For Callie was a bit too vain –
Her ego in the tyrant vein,
And those who knew her thought it best
To show her how she has oppressed

All those who felt her wrath and hate
And suffered as she'd denigrate
The choices that they'd made with care
For Callie's taunts were tough to bear

And so, they planned a special day
But what she saw the fifth of May?
We'll never know, for she won't tell
What Callie found in her own hell.

Elaine Person

Urgent Care Recommendations
(or how to write an upbeat poem about a bad situation)

Rockports, no sports
Rest and relaxation
Can't dance, no chance
I need medication.

Bed rest, my test
Could I please stay still?
Can't walk, just talk
I'm over the hill.

Injury all over me
Why did this thing happen?
Too much pain on my brain
I think that I'm snappin'.

Can't wait 'til I'm great
And active once again
They say pain will go away
They just don't know when.

Diane Reitz

Gone Too Soon

Rain, muddy path to light
early morning to starry night
Rhythm river, ocean bound
hardly lost and barely found
Puddles of footprints
imprinted the land
gone too soon
in a shifting sand.

Rosa C. Rodriguez

The Hug of Time

The air whispers
In the ears of time.
Everything is enclosed
In the global capsule,
That forms the feelings
And emotions of mankind.
The crude and rough sound
Of the gigantic ocean
Sings the sweetest dreams
That feed the night,
Announcing the arrival
Of the new dawn.
The breeze
transforms the storms
In peaceful days of love.
gravity suspends
The silent steps of the world
Where every day
People try to climb ...
Ascending and descending,
To finally get trapped,
In the hug of time.

Lynn Schiffhorst

I Feel For The Devil

Placed under Enemy mandate
To say the wrong thing forever
To make his best presents to heroes
And get them sent back unopened,
To tuck himself into small, wet, repellent shapes
Smelling of stagnant ponds,
Obliged by theatrical custom
To "exit demon weeping,"
To wrap himself up in draggle-tailed wings
And cringe with a grimace of chagrin
When holy water hits him like spittle.

Carolynn J. Scully

Courage

Search the weary, pain-filled face
of one who never gives place to the enemy,
and discover courage.

Look into the center of battle
where the unshackled draw weapons
and their future holds up courage.

People desire courage
witnessed in the steps of
brave souls, yet,

despise the need for strong minds
when we, ourselves, are enveloped
in a place where courage is birthed in us.

Thus, we look into weary, pain-scarred hearts,
treasure small victories,
and are encouraged.

Lyn Sedwick

Ars Poetica

These lines I know you've heard before,
They're good enough to hear once more.
"In the room the women come and go,
Talking of Michelangelo."

Some poems are simple, their rhymes delight,
Mixing sound and sense, terse and tight:
"A right jolly old elf and I laughed when I saw him,
In spite of myself."

I look for poems whenever I can,
Some fill your soul, some only your hand.
"One fish, two fish, red fish, blue fish."

My poems have no ruffles or frills,
And they're written on screens, not with pencils or quills.
"In Xanadu did Kubla Khan
A stately pleasure dome decree,
Where Alph, the sacred river ran,
Through caverns measureless to man,
Down to a sunless sea."

When rhyme and rhythm and word unite,
Their combination makes meanings ignite:
"Swept with confused alarms of struggle and fight,
Where ignorant armies clash by night."

I like poems that tell me a story or two,
Sometimes they're so good they sing it to you.
"There was a virus going round, Papa caught it and he died last spring,
And now Momma doesn't want to do much of anything."

And I like to think if I'm lucky to be
Alice and well at one hundred and three
Poems will still be singing to me.
"I wake to sleep, and take my waking slow.
I learn by going where I have to go."

Juli Simon

Hurricane Season

The radio sputters like wet clouds shouting,
while the candle burns.
The world has, in all ways, gotten smaller.
We hold up the house; our backs against
the hallway walls.

We are willing our favorite tree, so close to the house,
to be strong; hold tight.
We are calm, though there are no children
who need to be reassured by our bright faces.
They are far and away in colleges, knowing their own
and separate fears, but not this hurricane.

Gusts and swirls toss branches and leaves, sounding
wetly heavy.
The dogs are restless; they lie down, then pace,
then quiet. They seem to settle until a mass made of
rattle and movement churns above our roof.

All the mercies left in the world
are here in this small space.
We are holding hands, busy being amazed,
then absorbed in the tingling quiet.

It's only rain.
Until the wind wakes up.

Shelley Stocksdale

Birds Roost

My family was brought at last together
after being far apart for so long
by this friend of fine plumage and feather
we took ear to his cry playing his song.

From sage heron we talked of owls and trees
and then moved on to faces and places.
It's fun playing memory in the breeze;
steals fresh away from cat and mouse chases.

Oh, old great blue, you've brightened our grey day.
We looked over lake, you flew into view,
wrapped your nest 'round us in every way.
Crisp thinking, smooth talking through you imbued.

More and more often, let's call to big bird.
You flap wings while we wag tongue into word.

Emily Sujka

Overcomplicated

All the things complicated,
Simplified.
All the incompletes,
Nullified.
All the fears?
Mummified.

Dr. Jenni Sujka

10 Years From Now

They always ask the question:
Where do you see yourself in 10 years?
No one thought to say living through a pandemic,
Missing a graduate school graduation,
18 hour drive away from family,
And heartbreak…again.

No one tells you the inner pain and loneliness
That begins to swell with bills and hardship
Body falling apart faster than an ice cream cone
In sweltering Florida heat.

At 30, you will start to feel old they say.
A sense of dread kicks my youth to the floor
And won't stop kicking in fury.
Waiting for the light of safety,
But it never comes.

Stan K. Sujka

Memories

Like the ocean
Memories run in and out
Our prints in the sand are gone
But —
Time together
Will never be erased

Mark Andrew James Terry

For Sister Twinkle

The summer-sun that growth bestowed
enkindles on this journey's road
an ember glow from long ago
transmitting amber-flickered throw.

I know this life exacts a toll,
and takes control, insisting role
that keeps we two so far apart,
but summertime inflates my heart
and lifts it high on grateful wings,
reminding me, when I was foal,
that you were there in apron strings
to mentor me, and too, console.

A warm inviting sense of place
exists in me, there by your grace,
where stars and moonbeams interlace
and memories are upper case.
It's there I look for comfort's face
and see that smile I long to trace.

Cheryl Lynn West

Lyman Lee Home

Old house, the men are waiting.
They come to tear your bones apart,
remove you from the land where
you stood from one century to another.
It's hot. They have no care for you,
just a job, cash collected at sunset.
But I know you, saw your arrival
by mule train, down a dirt path
widened by cattle and Cracker horses
through Mascotte and Mabel
on their way to market on Tampa docks.

Those biscuits, their smell mingled with
the smoke of wrapped cigars,
men rocking on the porch.
It was the end of a long day, a rough ride,
cattle grazing through the night.
Early morning, the men filled saddlebags,
biscuits still warm from the oven.

You stood but trucks replaced horses
and drivers no longer stopped.
Families came and went, each
with less desire to care for you,
vandals and thieves the last
to enter your doors.

I watched you, heard you cry
as your roof, rusted, seeped red
into your cracking sides.
Windows shuttered, released a sigh,
the porch, once resting spot
of kin and neighbors,
tumbled from your grip.

The men are gone, as are you,
but others came, collected
your scattered bones.
They gave you breath, so you may
live again—a new barn raised,
polished floors where small feet trod.
Furniture, handmade and painted,
sits upon another porch
where travelers rest along this road.

Shari Yudenfreund-Sujka

The Peach

Your fragrance wafted over to me,
As I passed you in the store.

So sweet and intoxicating,
I could not have wanted you more.

In my home you ripened to perfection.
Soft and fragrant with that deep cleft in your side,

Juicy and tasty was your blood red streaked fruit.
I could have not been more satisfied.

POETRY FOR
THE LOVE OF IT

Laurence Amuso

De Naturibus

You can only make a first impression
once
in a while cupidity arises as suddenly
as the sun peeks from behind
dark clouds
obscure vision and gets one into the quick of
destructive actions
beget reactions of hateful
reconciliation
often brings another round of
dissension
leaves man betwixt virtuousness and malevolence

Sue Hansen

Sorta Rap

Hey, mon ami
Don't you cater to me
I have no intention
Of becoming your invention
Don't try no intervention
We together all these days
Don't make me change my ways.

You know my imperfections
Ain't sent in your direction
So jus' lay back and listen
Stead of just insistin'
On your own point of view

Cause this climate change is new
And I tell you that if you
Can't see things
In this new light
Then for sure there'll
Be a huge fight
Yeah, that's in sight
So with all our might
we gotta get it right
hang tight and get it right.

Louise Pare-Lobinske

on mom's first heavenly birthday

"wonder why loss feels more like theft"[1]

she read,
on the day it made a year
since we lost mom

it did feel like theft
between the dementia and the death

i cry
useless tears of pain
aching in the knowledge
i could have had more time with her
had she only been sound

i dream about her
almost every night
she speaks to me as ever
of things that matter and that don't
        in daylight she appears to me
ever at my side
ready with a hug and an "i love you"
hands of comfort on my shoulders
i feel her love
almost as if i could still touch her
she is always here
and i am always grateful

this is what life is, isn't it
loss

but the people i've lost
made me who i am
they are ever a part of me
i carry them with me always

the guilt i feel over
enjoying my alone time with dad
is for another day

today is for remembering
and loving
my one and only mother
who once gave up heaven for me
        but next time heaven asked for her,
she said, "i'm ready now"

enjoy your beloved rest, mom
you've earned it

[1] from the poem Requiem: "Laying to rest the souls of the dead things like a
name, like a dream, like a sin, like a parent" by Alora Young

Linda Whitefeather

"Good-bye"

Drifting off to sleep, I hear their calls
I see them circling the waters
Wings spread wide drifting on wind
In my inner vision
Gulls over the gulf
Searching, seeking
As I say
"Good-bye,
Friend"

SPACE COAST POETS

Nancy K. Hauptle MacInnis

This American Has A Dream

This American has a dream
Her people begin to see the unseen
Honor Spirit Holy dwelling within
Who hovers without one another's skin
Circles the entire social spectrum
With love in arms, hope to all a welcome
A door to each living being swings free
Inhale first breath toward sweet eternity
Free to exhale their last breath unto death
In between live the glorious present
With an eye to a fortunate future
Heart to where the historic past so went
To hear you are free to try, free to fail
To receive a conviction, receive a "Hail!"
Yes that we would begin to understand
When to let exist, when to let just be
When to lend a hand, when to intercede
Dreams of unity sown among red blood
Purity of peace as the white rose bud
Growing taller under sun's golden warmth
Blue skies of justice over head and hearth
Dance bright as a dark night's stars do sparkle
Bold, strong shadows behind cool glow of moon
Oh yes! And no it can't come too soon!
This American has a dream
Her people now see beyond the unseen
Promise wholly spectacular to know
Spirit Holy technicolor rainbow...

Anne-Marie Simonton

Ritual

Black birds gather
in an amber field
hovering over one another
in a strange dance
their harsh incantations
defiling the air,
molesting the earth,
raping the morning
of its beauty.

In a nearby tree
a dappled bird
begins to sing
an ancient melody
its cheerful voice
clamoring
against the wind
dispels
the obscene rite
from our earthly gathering.

SUNSHINE POETS

Angie M. Mayo

The Stranger in the Mirror

There
she is.
The woman
in the mirror
appears familiar.
Yet I question… who's she?
Seems not long ago she was
a young girl, sunlight in her hair.
But now, the shine is no longer there.
And also gone are the natural curls.
The radiant blush of her cheeks turned sallow.
There's no glow: the effect of the years.
From once full lips, lines radiate,
evidence of countless smiles.
The woman sighs and stares
so I turn around
and walk away.
She does too.
We'll meet
soon.

Cheri Neuman Herald

Lessons From Lockdown

I'd use the time well
get lots of things done
the country locked down
was no time for fun.
I sorted the Tupperware
homecooked my meals
burned some old paperwork
searched ebay for deals.
Polished the silver
trimmed my own hair
purged all the closets
of clothes I don't wear.
Then I slowed down
stopped watching the time
slept a bit later
began a new rhyme.
Sat on the porch
and noticed the birds
listened to music
and heard all the words.
The quiet is lovely
without all the cars
I laze with the cats
and gaze at the stars.
Learned that my days
are sweeter spent slow
It took a pandemic
to learn what I know.

TOMOKA POETS

B.J. Alligood

My Constellation

My son, my daughter,
my sisters, my brother,
even my deceased parents —
these are the beings that have
been my constellation for years.
As sure as the sun rises each
morning they have been there
to illuminate my path through life.

They have guided me, loved me,
influenced me, inspired me.
They have encouraged me,
motivated me, lifted me, and
nursed me.

They have cheered me through
challenges and provided comfort
through losses. They have laughed
with me through life's capriciousness
and shared amazement at its beauty
and gifts.

They have been my beating heart
in times of darkness and loss
as well as my lifeboat during
rough seas.

I have been blessed beyond
imagination to have a galaxy
of friends and family that have
surrounded me, buoyed me,
and supported me through life.

Thank you, each and every one.

Gary Broughman

Watering Weeds

It's a first step at least,
to give up watering the weeds,
to stop inhaling poisoned air,
to resist drinking water
I know is tainted before
I lift the cup to my lips.

I will leave the weeds to wither
and give my days to walking
where Beauty reigns,
among flowers no one
could mistake for weeds,
where the air whispers hope
and clear waters bubble with
Eternity's promise,
where words do not cut, but heal.

People say weeds can be pulled up
and thrown beside the road for
men in a green truck to gather,
never to return. It's true—
people do say that.

For now it's enough that weeds
get no more help from me.

Breathing in, I smile,
breathing out, I give thanks.
Breathe in, breathe out.
For now, it's enough.

Niki Byram

Surfer Jack and The Enchanted Forest

You look so young, your face so smooth,
I don't think you even shave, a man-child still …
Yet, you're so very cool.

Riding your surfboard, you're right at home,
Comfortable, on your home turf.
You tackle all the crashing surf,
Those wicked rips, waves and swells.

As you forge on ahead of me, I call you brave!
When we surf together, you're trying to find yourself.
Me, I'm trying to forget who left me behind.
Each of us now reaching for and
Relying on one another.

You know I'm trying to come back
From a broken heart,
I don't want to break yours in return,
Because I care so much for you and
You're there for me at every turn.

You're my knight in shining armor,
Arriving on your wooden steed,
Riding to me on the waves,
In my time of need.

I want you to be able
To follow the sun,
Riding atop the waves,
And not take a tumble.
Yet, you knew I was ready for
Your magic after my dreams crumbled.

You said, "I'll take you to the enchanted
Forest and never let you return to before."
Knowing we will have to part
At some hazy date in the future
I'll always keep you with me,
In my heart forever,
Because I love you more.

Mitzi J. Coats

Refugees

The numbers explode as they wait,
10,000, 100,000, 630,000, millions more,
a human train plodding to safer ground
pleading for food a place to sleep to belong,
in newspapers television radio internet
the stories similar yet each their own ...

"We creep as quietly as we can from camp
to well (spring, river) many kilometers away,
careful not to sniffle or clank buckets.
The killers (the enemy, insurgents, rebels)
crouch in the dark behind bush (forest, desert)
like panthers ready to spring upon their prey.
Girls, we are just girls. Not yet marriage age.
Our fathers became soldiers, conscripted to
fight against others like themselves. Or if they
refused, massacred before we ran from our
village, their heads pitched on poles to warn
sons and brothers who would revenge them.
Our mothers' bellies swell with violently planted
seed, babies unlike us who will be born into
a war of no meaning and know nothing else.
This night, we slip back into our tent, (lean-to,
cave) unheard, untouched. Why they let us return.
we don't think about. We twist on straw pallets,
(leaves, dirt floors); our eyelids quiver at every
noise: tree limbs snapping, insects singing.
Should we wake again to sun warming us
through the cracks, we will dig roots, trap small
rodents to silence the rumbling of our neverending
hunger. At any moment we will flee this shelter,
edge closer to the next border (ocean, mountain,
country). The water in our filled buckets will
quench our thirst for another day. And we wait"

... the world first welcomes them opens its arms
to them, then stretched to limits of relief, afraid
of the spreading virus of despair, closes its gates
turns them away debates their futures, while they
wait the numbers implode allowing accepting
less 12,000, 1000, 100, one family

3rd Honorable Mention, The Peace Award, 2016 FSPA

Sonja Jean Craig

Seed Song

With the breath of the wind
I float across the sky
       effortlessly
            in total surrender.

Cradled by
       a dancing breeze
I carry the Seed of Life
over manicured neighborhoods.

Across the busy streets
the inertia of the speeding cars
       lifts me to the highest
           aero acrobatics of joy.

In a wooded clearing
I rest on the
       welcoming ground,
warmed
       by a shaft of golden sunlight.

Fairies sing the song of my flower
coaxing my seedling to thrive,
       a flourishing blossom
           I dream alive.

Marc Davidson

Snare Drum Weather

Summer is hot
as the sun beats down
and the rainstorms soak
afternoons

But the wind will blow
and the crops will grow
though we all get burned
all too soon

Fall descends
and the leaves come down
and the harvests pass
in the fog

But a pumpkin's grin
brings the joy back in
as the children play
with the dog

Winter harsh
brings the icy cold
that will make us numb
in the day

Though we warm by fires
we express desires
for the quick return
of next May

And the Spring brings rain
and the warmth we seek
and the green world sprouts
tiny shafts

Though the roof may drum
when the spring rains come
and we all catch cold
from the drafts.

The full year round
there is weather's bite
to discomfort us
with its storms

We must last it out
and we must not pout
for it bounds our lives
with its forms

Linda Eve Diamond

Unwritten

This is where an unwritten poem began about...
whatever it was — when someone *popped in* —

the *worst* person to appear at such a time,
my future self, claiming she's here to help

arriving uninvited, leaning casually
and deliberately on the delete key...

Really?? Is that the best you can do?
You'd look back on that and cringe.
delete *delete* *delete*

... as if that weren't enough, I feel my past self
looking over my shoulder, shaking her head...

Really?? Is this what you do now?
Nothing here seems quite right.
delete *delete* *delete*

until there's nothing left and this
is where that poem would be

but it isn't—and I guess
it's for the best.

Mary-Ann Westbrook

What And Where

In the here and now
Then and There have
come and gone

Now and then we
wonder how and why
they disappeared

What and Where asked
High and Low to help
search for them

Who and Whom said
Then and There are
lost in the

come and gone and
can never be
here and now

Sometime What and Where
Might be come and gone
Perhaps they will find

Then and There and
can talk about the
when and where
over a cup of tea

Brown Pelican at Rest, New Smyrna Beach.
Daniel L. Stone.

MEMBERS AT LARGE

JG Annino

Lucky

To seek out your short story,
portal to adventure.

To inhale your novel at pink morning into day
blue skies day overtaken by full flower moon night.

To fall into your poem,
release for tears.

To mention your memoir:
"You. Must. Read. This."

To like your limerick. It made
made my laugh, last.

To grab torn envelope's backside
scribble a poem

Which I woke up without, and now
will ever keep.

Swati Bagga

Life

The precious pulse of "Being"
The tender act of Thriving, Knowing
Sprouting forth in the tiny cracks
of the bustling Highways
Leaning, tumbling, reaching for support
As the bloody hands craft a dead end.

Sometimes trickling and then gushing
Throbbing and pulsing – it passes us by
And we stand at it's Doorway - mute as strangers.
Live! We hear, the Clarion call
In our perplexed Medley of thoughts
So we run, we push, we jostle with one another
And Cry out, "I know. I am."

In the rush hour did we step on that
Tiny sapling just raising it's frail green head?
And oh! The bird that winged by, was it green or red? Or?
"whatever" - we said.
How much of the Earth do we carry with us we ask

"Yay not much by any chance" – we shrug.
Going Dull going Blind we crawl by
in this Life as spectators aloof.

Living a lost cause in this arid life
Where The Mountains bleed and the Rivers whimper
the Oceans choke and the Air cries foul
And the Trees burn and scream,
"Save us Save us Oh! Magician".
And we let it all pass by like the roll of some thunder
For we say " I Know, I am."

Life flows by this very moment in that
Gentle cascading stream,
In those washed pebbles underneath
In that warm joyous caressing sun ray
And the ambient green and blue of this Earth.

And we stand and stare blank
Contriving- was it too late for a Second Chance
Did the Fair of life call Curtain Drop?
As we sat still amidst the empty rows of chairs
In the Theatre of the "I know, I am."

Pat Bastendorf

Mixed Cinquain

water
running downhill;
avoiding deep puddles
taking the least resistant path
that's me.

water
percolating
finding its own level
happy to be mixed with others
that's *you*.

water
separated
into different liquids
can't be real; but mixed together
that's us.

Hanh Chau

Dew Drop

A fresh dewdrop like a teardrop
                Falling from its eyes
Displayed through the
                tiny crystal silver drops
lingering on the exquisite soft petal rose
                quenching the green thirst flourish leaf
through the early misty morning rise
                waiting for the gentleness caressing
To refreshing from its cleansing touch
                Ease away the misery bitterness frosty cold
With a warmth nurturing sun bright
                To bring joy and delight to the new day
With a reviving hope and embrace
                To uplifting the weary soul

Christine Cock

Ode to the Paddle Fan

Warm air twirls   a lazy vortex
                    in a Cat-on-a-Hot-Tin-Roof kind of way—
                              an essence of the almost-touch of sex
tic   tic   tic   throughout the day

A feathered breeze strokes my flesh
                    from toes to head   flat paddles circle
                              reaching creases   wafting fresh
in my own hot spiraling thermal

Groin   arms   legs   neck
                    oh   dearest fan   cool this sheen of sweat
                              oscillations keep internal heat in check
slightly off balance   my best lover yet

Barry A. Dimick

A Summer Night

A two-run double moved
the visitors into a five-four
lead at the top of the
final inning.

The count stood at three balls,
two strikes in the bottom of the
inning. Runner on first. Cool
clear air enveloped the baseball field.

A barge canal separated Cape Cod from
mainland Massachusetts. Tonight, the
cool air formed thick fog rising high above the water,
looking gray beyond the right and center field lights.

Shouts of encouragement burst from the
dugout: "Let's go!" "We need two." "Hit
another home run for the win." The team
support felt good. Helped to calm me.

Anxiety on both sides. "Strike him
out,"—from the visitor's bench. "Good location."
"Strike him out!" And many other comments.
Can't blame them, really.

I stepped back into the batter's box. Settled
down. Shut out all sounds. Focused on the
pitcher's right hand. He wound up and
threw the ball.

Fastball on the inside. Meat to me. Heard the sharp
crack of the bat. I watched the ball sail out of the park
as I rounded first base. Approached second as the ball
carried into the fog ... far beyond center field.

Shouts, greetings at the plate. High fives and slaps on
the back. I'd hit a home run with the game on the line.

Yay!

Melody Dean Dimick

Marianna Reform School

Blood on the walls,
Grinding of the old fan,
Bedsprings singing a child's blues.

One-armed man swinging,
Beating with the leather strap.
Blood on a child's flannel pajamas.

Dig, dig, dig.
Three holes behind the chow hall,
Four feet deep and as long as a boy.

Blood drips from the Sunshine State.
In court, justice moves sloth slow.
One hundred years of hell exposed.

"Consider the whistle blown,"
Leon County judge decreed.
Sundown on the Dozier School for Boys.

Ann Favreau

The Glassblower

A sweaty artist with hollow pipe
Gathers a glowing mass
From the fiery furnace.

An orange orb
From the glory hole
Clings to blowpipe's end.

He rolls, shapes
The sizzling sphere
With cherry blocks
And calipers of care.

Pursing his lips like a passionate lover
He breathes into the molten glass,
Opens the sweltering solid
Emancipates an exquisite form
My hands and eyes will caress.

Raymond Fones

Afterwards

At some point it all seems
afterwards, then the weight of memory—
the bright triumphs as fleeting
as deer spotted in a forest,
terrible moments that seem
to never end, the shining ones
that wrap around you
like a warm blanket
and beg to be recalled
over and over and over again.

An old stone farmhouse
one afternoon in early spring,
sunlight flooding in through
tall windows, the air cool,
a large room filled with friends
and friendly strangers,
green-stemmed wine glasses,
a pot of chili on the stove
and you, there on the couch,
graceful, queenlike,
legs curled comfortably beneath you,
accentuating a reply
with a simple, elegant
gesture of your hand.

Charles Hazelip

What Makes a Friend a Friend?

Our friends are people we like to be with.
     Hopefully,
they often like to visit us as well.

A friend may be recently found
        somewhere,
Or imbedded deeply in our life-tale.

Old friends enjoy warm regards
       recalling memories from decades ago
           and places known so well.

A friend shares our beliefs and insights
       or maybe
           just respects choices we make.

Friends overlook flaws they see
       because
           they think our friendship is worth it.

Good friends are those whose absence we miss.
       Their departure
           leaves our lives un-whole.

Previously published in *Good Things Good People Ponder*, 2020

Nina Heiser

Orange Juice

An open can of Minute Maid
A spoon planted in orange tundra
On the freezer door
At Ellen's house
Help yourself it said
Whenever you are ready for me

We drank fresh-squeezed at my house
My mother pressing citrus halves
For every spit of juice, we drank
From small indigo glasses only
At breakfast our oranges ordered
From the Indian River Fruit Company

Wearing a long white nightgown
Her hair plaited and placed against her breast
Ellen's mother wandered through a chaos
Of growing children on couches
In a room where living was allowed
Feasting on frozen

Loving spoonfuls
Reveling in negligence
I am here
When you want me

Dr. Emory D. Jones

Deep Freeze

I am not going to say it is cold,
But when you milked the cows,
They gave ice cream,
And you could knock over
Any frozen goat.

The chickens hatched penguins,
And the horse snorted
Ice-sickles.

The windows of the house
Glazed over,
And as the inside heat
Melted the ice,
It became running rainbows.

The thermometer
Plunged to ten below zero,
And the trees exploded
Like cannon shots.

Now that was cold,
And if you believe me,
I will tell you another
Tall tale.

Judith Krum

The Line Between

love must be an act of truth-telling
stained with the sweet, grave weight of ink
— *Rachel Kaddish*

Where on the page does love grow?
Where on the page does love end?
The ink tells the story, marking the line
Between truth and lie.
The page is cream vellum, slightly scratchy,
Slubbed to catch the ink in its tiny potholes.
Where the ink flows is where truth is told.
Textured words from fountain pens,
The nibs move easily over nubby sheets
Marking the places where words speak truth.
Pithy reminders of consequences and frustrations,
Pigment imbedded with smooth strokes,
Archival quality black silk
Spread across the metaphors of life.
Sincerity quilled, spilled, streaked, smudged,
Then blotted with bibulous paper
Absorbing the excess,
Wicking away love's truth.
Thus, on the page love grows.
Thus, on the page love ends.

Cheryl Licata

Untimely Unity

My dog and I visited a dear lady
last week at the nursing home.
We exchanged smiles.
Our eyes locked momentarily.

She asked my dog's name.
I told her Murphy.
Delight shone on her face
as her hand reached out

to touch the soft hair
and peer into my dog's soul,
the same, almost thoughtful gaze
she bestowed on me.

As if, for a brief instant
there was a hazy memory,
Recognition of someone ...
somewhere ... sometime ...

We have introduced ourselves
once a week for seven years.
Each time she asks my dog's name
and we share the same stories.

After a few moments
she grows tired of petting.
Murphy and I move on,
knowing we will meet anew next week.

Mary Ellen Orvis

On the Beach in Northern Ireland

I walk along the Antrim strand.
Sand blows across the grassy dunes.
Small channel waves froth, rush in.
Shell bits surround footprints glistening.
They've traveled far, now take a rest
beneath the gaze of dimpled cliffs.

Who shall tend me when I'm gone?
Dress me up and lower me down?
A pauper's grave, a burial at sea?
An ashy urn to comfort me?
Shall friends enjoy an Irish wake
where whiskey flows and thirst is slaked?

I stroll across the Irish shore,
watch boys toss sticks for man's best friend.
Nearby graffitied levee reads:
One crown, one Queen, no Pope!
For me:
a mackerel sky endomes the beach.
I sigh — it is just beyond my reach.

[3rd Place, The Tomoka Poets Award, 2020 national competition sponsored by the Florida State Poets Association]

Dennis Rhodes

Stopping by the Sea on a Rainy Evening
Parody of Robert Frost's Stopping by Woods on a Snowy Evening

Whose beach this is I can't deny:
it belongs to some hedge fund guy.
He will not see me stopping here
to watch the sun fall from the sky.

My little dog must think it odd
to stop this way. He gives a nod
and tugs so gently on his leash
while his owner communes with God.

He shakes the raindrops from his head
wanting to get home to bed
but ultimately lets me be
and lifts his leg to pee instead.

The sea is lovely, deep and blue
but I have many things to do
and blocks to go before I'm through
and blocks to go before I'm through.

Al Rocheleau

On Vengeance

Marlowe Meeting a Betrayer

Since I am dirt in memory spread without
The drab and subtle curtsy of a stone,
Do not fear me!
Wonder without wondering when or if
The knocker's answer comes to call—
Remember one of years, of decades thence,
One you cannot place for here when there
In mention mingles treason with defence!
This figure, scarred and bearded in its measure
Of the old, or older such, a cold aquaintance?
More, do you believe in ghosts, in jests,
In incomes come in justice for injustices
As Judas spent, to hang in this, this moment,
Do not fear me!
I am the personage the play erased,
Restored and just before the black, you hear me.

Mary Rogers-Grantham

Graves of Sand

Everything is said. Everything is said again.
Everything hurts. Everything hurts again.
Civility and violation unbutton cloaks of wrath.

Too many pending investigations, again.
Too many justified police killings, again.
There is merit in all the colors of sand.

A global pandemic quilts colorful world protests.
A global pandemic summons delayed protests.
Buried stones and ornamental conduct incite voices.

While weathering change on a shuffling ladder,
while breaking the sun and pulling the wind down,
we inhale your name and we exhale your name.

Death is a metaphor shaping history.
Death is a cavern that covers midnight.
It is genesis dipping shade without shape.

Everything is said. Everything is said again.
Everything hurts. Everything hurts again.
Our hearts beat with wounded syllables.

To be continued. Continued. Continued…

Evelyn Ann Romano

La Mer

My eyes sing as I near

the sea, white light pulls

me close, I step into bliss,

feel with the third eye.

My body a hand in the sea's

velvet glove, flow woven

in gentle waves, patient pace

of morning air, musician's

mantle of soft chords. Mint,

anise, lemongrass part my

lips, brush my tongue. My

body buoyed by this

ancient element:

a missing lover,

a homecoming.

Published in the Sandhill Review, 2019

Juliana Romnes

The Calm Before

The air is brisk, yet the sun feels warm
and there isn't a cloud in the piercing blue sky.
But the grass is buried under powdery white snow
because I'm living in a snow globe
and my world is about to be shaken.

Tim Schulz

Heart Strings

She was the love of his life
until she no longer was
cast aside seemingly forgotten
Oh how she longs for his touch
his fingers caressing her neck
the feel of her lithe body
pressed tightly against his
and the parties with friends
music filling the night until
the light of the next day
sounds of the Dobro in
harmony with soulful vocals
of course the fiddle and banjo
a Dulcimer with its quirky looks
and the ever present flat top
then there was her
the sexy mandolin
producing such sweet sounds
her strings bending to his will
deriving pleasure from fulfilling
his every desire, his every whim
now feeling very much unloved
In the dark closet alone
locked in her case, latched tight
forced to endure hearing it all
him and her, the new one, such nerve
what has hurt him so, she hears the pain
sorrow resonating from every note
this new lover the Stratocaster
seducing him to play the blues
straying from his mountain roots
forsaking the music of his people
shunning her his first true love
she had noticed a change subtle at first

after that wretched trip to the Delta
surely he'll find his way back to Bluegrass
a click of the latch a sliver of light
her strings go taut in anticipation
as she's cradled once more in his arms

Daniel L. Stone

Summer's Almost Gone

Translucent skies above
leaves begin turning different colors
and smoke rings drift in the air.
There is a golden glow
as the sun sets to rest, until tomorrow.
Autumn is blowing in
with the north wind .

There are now clear night skies
yet the moon looks framed in a hazy wreath.
Stars shine brightly to and from heaven.
Coolness is wrapping around me
musty dampness smells sweet
as the night brings a chill in the air.

Now night falls early
in the morning there is mist on my windows.
Dew now greets the morning sun
while creeks run rocky and shallow.
Again today the storm clouds threaten to rain.

Fall brings a warm kiss goodbye to summer
for something that is not the same as yesterday
and will not be the same tomorrow.

Summer's almost gone.

Daniel R. Tardona

Life in a Cardboard Box

Open space among concrete and crime
A whimper in the sunlight glow
Surrounded by urban waste and grime
In the cold of day and night they lay
Alone

With no family or friend to care
Peering out their cardboard home
People only pass and stare
Each day only lived to
Remain

Tortured souls that only seek a meal
No dreams to follow or to gain
To find a place to rest and heal
Each moment a time to bear
And find a place to rest and heal
Hoping tonight there is no
Rain.

Tanya R. Whitney

A Single Red Rose

Rooms sit empty, abandoned in life.
A chandelier sways in the wind
blowing through the broken windows.
Its chains creak from the movement.
Paint peels from forgotten walls
no longer holding memories
of those who once lived and loved
in the confines of the deserted chambers.

A bed frame stands tilted on three metal legs.
Its coils rusted and bared to the elements.
The only piece of furniture remaining
from its previous human inhabitants.
Forlorn and forgotten, no longer in use.
Rubble litters the floors like a shag carpet.

For thirty years it has sat empty.
Slowing eroding with time and weather.
Its exterior bearing the brunt of its decay.
Overgrown with brush and brown weeds,
a ghostly play area that will no longer hear
the laughter of children racing through there.

Once, louvered shutters hung loosely from
their mounts, swaying like drunken sailors
on shore leave after six months at sea.
A bicycle leans against the decayed
fence planks that once stood straight and aligned.
A place where life once prevailed and triumphed,
where love was unrivaled and celebrated daily,
now devoid of life, love, and celebrations
A single red rose peeks out the broken trellis.
Its lattice works pocked with opened spaces.
A symbol of rebirth in this lifeless place.
A sign that even in the most desolate
of places, life can survive and flourish.

Lady Liberty Replica, Orlando
Elaine Person

CHANCELLORS

Silvia Curbelo

The Road Back

All she asked for was a clean
shirt and quiet and a safe place to land
All she asked for was a window
overlooking a stream, some
railroad tracks, or a road
a stone's throw from anywhere
All she wanted was a good book
like an island and a steaming
bowl of rice, white clouds
in the alley, white
stone lifted from her mouth
A song, a boat, a way of going
All she wanted was a field,
and snowmelt, and a river,
and the wisdom of sparrows
in the yard, their brief
precarious histories like a promise
no one expects to keep
And all she wanted was a clean slate
of sky like a freshly washed
handkerchief, a brightness
she could taste on her tongue,
and soft dirt, and a hillside,
and hands to let go

Denise Duhamel

From Here To Eternity

I crossed the wooden steps to the hot sand and ran
into the rip current, each toss and tumble, the opposite
of the massages you used to give. The fish and rocks, the sudden cold spots,
the seaweed slaps, a mouthful of salt. I flung myself
into the plunging breakers, their fierceness and froth, the terrible
twinkle of sun. *Batter my heart, backwash and trough. Fling me to the ocean floor.*
The surfers were out for kicks. The lifeguard blew a whistle—
shark alert. I fought the plunges and swells, kicking you again
though you had left me for good. I stewed, angry in this angry womb.
A board flew over my head. All went black,
and then I was reborn, Deborah Kerr ashore without her Burt Lancaster.
Embarrassment. Melodrama. Mouth-to-mouth with a stranger.
I crossed the hot sand and the wooden steps and wrapped
myself in a towel, having taken the beating, having sought it. Thank you, sea,
for spitting me back, delivering me.

From *Second Story* (University of Pittsburgh, 2021)

Carol Frost

How Music Came Into The City

From wild, half-peopled hills
I have brought to your streets
sixty-six birds, rare species
of hummingbird and frightened little finch
with their beaks sealed shut
so they would not be heard singing
until I arrived. I sewed them inside
my clothing, simple songs
past hearing for the days
when silent snow mocks stone
and loud voices voice
the wasted breath.
Already can you dream
the rubied merriment
when I open my coat
and unspool the ribbon
from their beaks;
and the heartbreak
when a sole bird falls earthward
as if from a golden tree?
Listen now for the key
of what has been—
a tiny magnitude pouring
myrrh and wind
onto the avenues,
rustle in the undertones.
It will take you back
to the hills and take
the hills away.

Lola Haskins

Dominion

We name the birds and think those are their names

    but our throats are helpless when calling flights pass over

    and we can't taste the earth that comes up with the worm in a robin's beak

    nor in the worst moments of our lives can we approach the way an owl sobs.

We analyze the sky using charts   one phenomenon at a time

    yet when light pierces the clouds like our visions of God we turn into

    open mouths and when that light enters us   no matter how much

    we want to keep it   because we do not have the tools we can never.

We wade through undergrowth whose leaves and sticks are our words for them

      but the nodules and stitchings on our ankles will always know more about plants

      than we do and we have no idea what to call the way trees dwarf us nor when

      we hold them how to interpret the patterns their barks leave on our cheeks.

We have stories but we cannot parse them so when we step on a seedling struggling

    through a crack we never think of Cain and Abel nor does the way water

    cascades towards us from high and ancient rock bring Rapunzel to mind

    nor when we look at the stars do we remember *As it was in the beginning*.

When will we understand that all our classifications are only attempted dust?

    That nothing pinned to a card is true? That sight and hearing

    and taste and our hearts and our brains and the tips of our fingers

    are like yellow butterflies? Reach for them and they are gone.

David Kirby

Man Catches Baby

A dozen women surround me on the museum steps,
        laughing and calling to each other in a language

I can't understand, and then one of them tosses me
        a baby. I'd been looking at Pissarro's "Hoar Frost,"

which baffled critics with its depiction of the shadows
        of trees that are themselves absent from the canvas,

their bafflement based on their assumption that
        the shadows are somehow less real than the trees.

But what is real? When I was a student, my roommate
        Dennis took me out drinking till dawn on my birthday,

and as we walked toward our apartment, we saw
        the guy from the bakery leave a box of pies

in front of a diner. Dennis picked up a cherry pie
        and said, *Look*, and when I looked, he pushed it

into my face, then peeled a strip of crust off
        my forehead and ate it, and we sat on the curb

and finished that pie and another to boot.
        The next morning, the doorbell rang, and there

stood two men in black suits. One of them
        showed me a card that said FBI on it,

and I thought, all this for a couple of pies?
        But they were looking for someone else.

What is a shadow? Nothing, you say. A lack of light.
        But what if the darkness came first and light interrupted it?

Pissarro's critics were less than thrilled: Jules Castagnary
        saw the absence of the trees as a "grave error,"

and Louis Leroy sneered that the picture consisted
        of "palette-scrapings placed uniformly on a dirty canvas . . .

neither head nor tail, top nor bottom, front nor back."
        Louis Leroy was overthinking it, wasn't he? You have

to see what you're looking at. When I caught the baby,
        the women moved in close, and one put her hand

inside my jacket, but I figured even a bad mother
        wouldn't drop her own child, so, yeah, I tossed it back.

Peter Meinke

An Old Soldier Soughing in the Dark

In my 88th year I've reached Bunyan's 'Slough
of *Despond*' an abandoned word a verbal hiccough
now while *Despair* hangs around on this ruinèd bough
forever and ever and the wind groans through
the oaks brushing our house pushing the tough
stems and acorns along the roof a ghosty plough
till they bounce down to the trough
below hacking the dirt trenches like a wet cough

But still l remember when on a night as rough
as this full of cheap wine and sourdough
bread you played a rinkydink piano and though
we were broke as gypsies I was on furlough
so we sang *O are you going to Scarborough*
Fair and my God we were happy or happy enough

Virgil Suárez

Vibrational Reciprocity

Doug Anderson, a poet I admire brings
to my attention the Coconut Monk,

"who lived on a floating island on the Mekong
with a huge statue of the Buddha on one end

and another huge statue of Jesus on the other."
Whose followers included American service men

who went AWOL during the war and to whom
the monk, being a pacifist, provided refuge.

I am reading about the Coconut Monk during
a graduate student's defense in musicology:

something about how vibrational resonance
affects the human voice, the *Duende's* blues .

I am 8 years old, I am standing by a huge 55 gallon
drum my father placed in the corner of the patio

to collect rain water so my mother could do
the laundry and wash the dishes. The storms

have passed. Drops fall into the filled drum.
Havana, Cuba 1970, Cuban military advisors

Fighting on the side of the North Vietnamese.
One drop at a time. One plops in and waves ripple

to the brim and return to the center. I see
a boat on a river carrying the remains of pacifists

who died waiting for that war and many others
to end. I see a man on a balcony get shot,

another on the floor of a California hotel kitchen
bleeding out, a man whispering not to let

go into his ear. Another drop. Like this poem
rippling into the world expecting something in return.

Ibis Committee
Sonja Jean Craig

FLORIDA STATE POETS ASSOCIATION ANNUAL POETRY CONTEST WINNERS

CATEGORY 1 FSPA FREE VERSE AWARD

Mary Rogers-Grantham
Palm Coast, FL

One Hundred and Thirty-Six

I come from a place where time slowly
simmered like a fresh cut of lean roast beef
in an unforgiving oven. I come from a place
where the audacity of weekday mornings
strummed my nostrils awake with the
arrogant aroma of roasted coffee searching
for a hot country breakfast.

Where Saturday morning sleep tasted like
fluffy homemade biscuits smothered in farm
butter and wild berry jelly with a side of
skillet fried red potatoes. Where Sunday
morning sleep tasted like a pitcher of ice
cold sweet tea, a few freshly squeezed
lemon slices floating like toy boats in a tub
of water. Where poetry basked in dialect and
culture emerged during family mealtime,
showed up during prayer time, and grew
wild in fields along highways.

I come from a place where I picked wild
blackberries by the gallon, walked barefoot
with scorpions and scaled trees that dared
me to fall. I come from a place where hours
in the dog days of summer moved at the
pace of a charming garden snail - no hurry,
no appointments - just navigating its destination.

I come from a place where the pride of
one hundred and thirty-six peace abiding folks
loved the smell of their Arkansas mountains.

CATEGORY 2 FSPA FORMAL VERSE AWARD (Ballad)

Holly Mandelkern
Winter Park, FL

Donne's Time and Our Time

You curse the ever present Sun
whose presence orders time.
You'd rather write the temporal rules
from bed, your clock sublime.

You hale the flea, a token priest,
who blessed your thoughts of union
the mingling of love's fluid flow,
love-making your communion.

But as our private moments mount,
we long to bound from bed.
Though love is strong, the days are long,
as are the books we've read.

We yearn for friends and family,
to flee from curtained room,
to walk the talk that freedom gives,
though grateful for our Zoom.

And do you search for sunlit joys,
confined to cloistered dreams?
Through airy windows, open doors,
we treasure sun-kissed beams.

Dear John, we're done with counting days
while coupled in a tent.
We'll measure time by Mr. Sun
whose climb greets our ascent.

CATEGORY 3 THE LIVE POETS SOCIETY AWARD

Stephen Stokes
Jacksonville, FL

Dry Run

The bath had gone cold.
She was lying back with eyes closed,
the water as still as gelatin
in which her body was sealed,
head resting on the lip of the tub,
listening to the faucet drip
with echoes that carried in the silence
like drops from a stalactite in a cave.
On the ledge of the tub a letter opener lay
beside a tiny bottle of red food coloring.

Her hand dripped as she reached
for the letter opener.
The drops tinkled as they struck
the water's surface.
Never having used the instrument on an envelope,
he having ended their relationship via email,
she ran the dull edge across
the babyish underside of her wrist,
the pink skin whitening along the slow stroke.

Upside-down over the water she squeezed
the tiny bottle that was like
the primer bulb on a lawnmower.
Black-looking drops unspooled
below the surface as red wisps.
She dribbled more food coloring,
watching the dark blobs turn red
and plume like smoke in air.

CATEGORY 4 THE TOMOKA POETS AWARD

Marc Davidson
Ormond Beach, FL

Ecclesia In Litore

Behold the new cathedral I attend.
Each Sunday morning early do I come.
To nature's preaching sermon do I bend
my ear, and to the surfs unhindered drum.
This sermon bids me understand the ways
in which my life should follow it through all
and tend my living to productive days.
The seabirds wheel and cry, response and call
The ocean's mighty organ plays above.
Bach's choral might in nature echoed well.
The service over, all depart in love
but still the organ plays in every swell.
    We go, and seek the good within our reach,
    who sought our place of peace upon that beach.

CATEGORY 5 WILLARD B. FOSTER MEMORIAL AWARD
(Etheree)

Sara Gipson
Scott, AR

Soup Kitchen

Soup-
simmered
chicken broth,
chips of fake meat,
chopped vegetables.
We serve with steam gifting
warmth to hands gnarled as aged oak,
to youths fresh as dew. Our faith hopes
to lift spirits from graves of despair.
Hungry homeless taste kindness in soupspoons.

CATEGORY 6 THE RONDEAU AWARD

Joyce Shiver
Crystal River, FL

Mother's Motto

Be always kind in all you do:
my mother's motto, plain and true.
    Through all her life her goodness showed.
    She never lost her kindness mode.
Her care and gentleness we knew.

A neighbor with a cold or flu
was helped with laundry, dinner, too.
My mother lightened every load.
    Be always kind.

A hungry man got soup or stew,
a little cash to see him through.
    Her cheerful helping never slowed,
    Time after time her kindness flowed.
A message here for me and you:
    Be always kind.

Robyn Weinbaum
Kissimmee, FL

Chris Dance

The first thing I saw when I woke was Chris' face
eyes still shut hovering on the inside
that bright orange; a Warhol Chris
pressed into my eyelid
haloed with blues and fours
calling me to dance
Chris' face, before the accident
before the crush of metal
before the diesel fire melted
asphalt and flesh into one
Chris' face and a slowly turning wheel

There is a ghost bike there
a tree swallowed part
gardenias drape the rest
At the turning of the year
I clean the leaves and spin
the wheel
still see Chris' face against the inside of my eye

I am old now; clippings are brittle
The ghost tree is tall grown through
the wheels don't spin
I sit on the roots
Chris dancing behind my eyes

Chris dancing
The last thing I saw before I slept
was Chris' hand
reaching for me to dance

CATEGORY 8 THE POET'S VISION AWARD

Joanne Vandegrift
Alva, FL

The Reverend Sandhill Crane

Reverend Crane stands preened and tall,
Ordained by his scarlet red cap.
His bugle call summons a flock
Of some who swim and those who flap.

An alligator, half submerged,
Is watching more than listening.
The fish, suspended in suspense,
Await the sermon opening.

Shrikes, perched on the "No Fishing" sign,
Await a breeze to set their pitch.
Today these two make up the choir
As songbirds who have found their niche.

White egret, great though thou maybe,
Perhaps your wetland pew too soft.
The frequent bobbing of your head
Suggests your spirit soars aloft.

Amen!

CATEGORY 9 THE NEW RIVER POETS AWARD

Beverly Smith-Tillery
Seminole, FL

Broken Promises

*LRMC - Landstuhl Regional Medical Center is the largest US military
hospital outside the continental United States. Located near Landstuhl,
Germany, it serves as the nearest treatment center for the wounded
soldiers from Iraq and Afghanistan. The acronym LRMC is pronounced
Larm-C.

I promised I would bring you home,
I pledged "no soldier left behind",
I thought that I could save you all,
But then I saw you slip away.
With skill and drugs and bags of blood,
I knew that I could pull you through.
But wounds so grievous, damage done,
It was impossible to save.
One day we'll meet again I know,
And then you'll say that you forgive,
That you knew how I tried so hard
And sometimes it is fate prevails,
But I can't let go of my guilt,
Of trying hard, but losing you.
The Army led us to believe,
That we could bring all soldiers home,
If they could get to LRMC's* doors.
It was a lie that I believed,
How foolish I was, just pipe dreams.
And now I deal with guilt and shame,
Because my promise was not kept.
And here is my advice to you,
Don't make a promise you can't keep.

CATEGORY 10 THE ALFRED VON BROKOPH AWARD

Stephen Stokes
Jacksonville, FL

Your Body's Footprint

Light sneaks in
between the linked slats
of the closed blinds.
You shuck the blankets
and leave a toasty pocket
in the abandoned bedding.
I scoot across
the meridian of the mattress
and settle into this nest.
The fabric there is kissed
with your skin's bouquet.
My head finds the hollow
yours made in the pillow.
The aroma of coffee
drifts into the bedroom,
overpowering the tinge of your scent.
I mash my face
into the pillow's scoop
and snort the last of you.
From inside your body's footprint
I hear the front door shutting.

CATEGORY 11 THE HOWARD & SANDY GORDON MEMORIAL
AWARD

Diane Neff
Longwood, FL

Mothering

"There's an upside to everything," she said,
when we were well into our third call of the week
with nothing to say, but the words kept coming
between us, comfortable, easy, familiar,
as we navigate this new world of no travel, no touch.
We can let our sentences run on,
no reason to stop with a period, using commas and dashes
between thoughts, circling back once, twice, letting it go,
picking it up again later when the other uses a particular word
and it reminds us of another detail.
How can you know your mother, I wondered,
without these conversations, 1200 miles apart
but more intimate than when we share a living room
and a meal? Reminiscing about a meal we had before,
while eating only what's in the cupboard today
because we don't make unnecessary trips
even to the grocery store. I worry that
she's eating crackers and mayonnaise,
or a piece of toast and apricot jam
with an expiration date seven months ago
that she just found in the back of the refrigerator.
I can't check, but I remind her to take care
of herself, to avoid falls and strains, and if it snows again,
to let the neighbors help shovel.
"You 're 90 years old," I reminded her, as if her arthritis
would let her forget. There is never an absence of pain,
never forgetting that she doesn't feel good
without qualification. But she soldiers on, that work ethic
she lives, embracing the struggle because it's her choice,
that driving motivation to always have choice, the belief
that once you allow others to help, you lose your choice
on how something is done, and you become either a shadow
fading into their identity, or an ungrateful witch

who doesn't appreciate sacrifices made on your behalf.
"Take care of yourself," I say again,
forbidding her to climb the ladder, promising to do it myself
when I get there, knowing that our lives would be
a more complicated tangle if she falls, knowing
that I will not be there in time before the ceiling bulb bums out,

CATEGORY 12
THE JANET BRINKLEY ERWIN MEMORIAL AWARD

Shutta Crum
Ann Arbor, MI

The Cat And I Look For Poems

In the fieldstone cellar
I run my fingers over hand-hewn beams
to find the cord still secured –
a smooth length of lifetimes – double-hitched.
Still pliable, this lifeline I've lashed to the house
leads us over little-used thresholds and
into darkened nooks. You do not complain.

We find boxes, partially crushed and stitched-up
with tape turning to dust. Opened, we brush the long years
from notebooks and admire the delicate traceries,
yellowed, soft-poems-some as intricate as Josephine Knots,
and just as tenacious. Others in which the silk,
spun from my body, have given way to tatters.

Still, I find summers here spent by unnamed lakes,
and fall days when you rolled in leaves the color of your fur.
There are winters with you and without.
And at our feet a tangled pile of springtimes.

In the quiet of the house, with you beside me, I trace
my fingertips over these needful indulgences,
once so delicately and diligently worked upon.
You help by jumping in and out of boxes –
a stalking paperweight, ready to pounce
should some crazed wind decide to invade the cellar,
unloose this lifeline and sweep away the lace of my life.

CATEGORY 13 THE NOAH WEBSTER AWARD

Catherine Moran
Little Rock. AR

Looking at the memorabilia

I glance around my rooms and seem to know
that the essence of my mother's glow

has been left to dwell in things she believed
might some quiet day be clearly perceived

by her daughter as worthy of some space.
In all her legacies I see the outline of her face.

She painted clustered flowers on the frame
of her antique mirror. It will proclaim

her love of creativity like a silent thought
in footsteps down my hall. I brought

her blue china vase from the top shelf
to a single table top. When I find myself

gathering jonquils and lilies to fill it up,
I remember her gardening. One painted cup

of hers waits on a hook just for my tea,
and several other things were left for me.

She gave me jewelry from the past
with shining memories content to last.

On more than one great family gathering
I've worn my mother's diamond ring

polished with the touch of soft memory.
It glimmers like a rhyme in poetry.

I've layered her wondrous string of pearls
and worn them to a luncheon with the girls.

And carefully I hook a silent silver heart
onto a slender chain. It contains a part

of us my mother cherished every day
A picture of my dead brother and me stay

in perfect locket pose. When I wear
jewelry she left, how much more aware

I am of her warm legacy. A little bit
of shiny metal and precious stones permit

me to begin to share her life. With delight
this memorabilia gives me such insight

into another person's fascinating themes.
I can only connect and add my own dreams.

Steven Leitch
West Jordan, UT

I Hate Chocolate

I saw her from a distance
happily walking towards
my docked boat
and lounging crew.

We just returned safely
from a long night's mission,
whole and untouched.

She had the same smile
she had when I gave her
my C-ration chocolate bar
before we left last night.

They were awful,
not like the Hershey bars
back home,
but she loved them.

Just a child,
six or seven at the most,
she wasn't the enemy,
yet what could I do.

She was walking, almost skipping,
with a stick grenade
placed under her arm
tight against her chest.

I yelled at her.
Du 'ng Lai! Du 'ng Lai!
Stop! Stop!

I hate chocolate.

Carolynn J. Scully
Apopka/Forest City, FL

Daddy-Daughter Dance

When she was young

he held her to his heart
waltzing to a heroic beat,
calming her baby tears,

caressing tiny fingers
with gentled strength,
guiding her unsure steps.

He was the Prince
gliding across the floor,
her feet atop his toes.

Tears masked by smiles
standing tall, announcing
dads' choice for proms' beauty.

Today she is not a child.
His flooded eyes blur
this vision in white;

a queen, now crowned
with another name.
He reaches for her hand,

leads her into the spotlight,
turns slow circles around
her graceful steps,

draws her close to his
tightened chest where
he wears his little girl's tears

one last time.

CATEGORY 16 THE PAST PRESIDENTS AWARD

Jerri Hardesty
Brierfield, AL

Oh By the Way, Which One's "Pink"

When David Gilmore steps upon a stage,
All ears are tuned entirely to him,
He lets his wild muse out of its cage
To play guitar like holy seraphim.
He pours out pleading notes and crying chords
And melodies that haunt the very soul,
Oblivious, it seems, to screaming hordes
Addicted to his brand of rock-n-roll.
I ride the wave of dripping liquid sound,
So lost in every rise and fall and bend.
His lilting art is where my joy is found;
I always wish his songs would never end.
His music has the power to transcend
In ways the heart, alone, can comprehend.

CATEGORY 17 THE CURRENT ISSUES AWARD

COL (Ret) Beverly Smith-Tillery
Seminole, FL

The End of War in Afghanistan

I heard it on the news today,
That finally we're coming home.
The war I fought for six long years
Is coming to its final end.
What did we gain in that sad place,
In desert plain and mountain pass?
We'd gain one step on Taliban
And then be pushed back twenty more.
We fought to make a better life
For all the children in that land,
But I feel that the day we're gone,
The things we built will tumble down.
And after twenty years I think,
What did we gain? What was the cost?

Cheryl A. Van Beek
Wesley Chapel, FL

Backdraft

My face presses against the scent of old pine.
The doorknob singes my fingers.
Eyelashes spider the keyhole.
Smoke balloons on the other side.
Is it the smoldering past, trapped in my eyes
burning through yesterdays like a diary ablaze?

What's on the other side -
the fog of a confused future rasping
in my throat, that curls under the door
like a cat's gray tail?
My fingers worry a skeleton key.
Sunlight burns through haze, breaks the seal.
The door bursts
open.

CATEGORY 19 LESLIE HALPERN MEMORIAL AWARD

Mardi Knudsen
St. Cloud, MN

Magic Story for Falling Asleep

When the last troll came out of the forest
and his bones turned to duff
and his clothes turned to saplings
nothing was left, but his hair,
which my mom took home
and knit into a warm blanket
which she tucks around me at night
when I dream of the last troll
when I fall asleep in the forest.

CATEGORY 20 THE HUMOR AWARD

Peter M. Gordon
Orlando, FL

CAT Scan Report

My lungs look like a ten year-old's,
So firm, so fresh, so clean.
Circulatory system's strong
and my aorta is pristine.

At the other end, my prostate's
large like a sewing machine.
Spine's shaped like a question mark,
but my aorta is pristine.

Fat liver could cause cirrhosis.
Rich food turns my skin green.
Colon's thicker where surgeons cut.
Still, my aorta is pristine.

Older I get, worse I look
on doctor's CAT scan screen.
Says I might live thirty more years
since my aorta is pristine.

For what purpose have I been spared?
Many friends have left this scene.
I promise to try to matter,
while my aorta is pristine.

CATEGORY 21 THE DORSIMBRA AWARD

Barbara Blanks
Garland, TX

Spring Jubilation

When April perches on my sill, it sings.
The mockingbird, with hallelujah trills,
helps raise the sun, while other life with wings
sips nectar-brimming cups of daffodils.

Woodpeckers drum
as robins warble,
and pigeons coo
freestyle madrigals.

While life is troublesome at times, I love
these spritely spring bouquets of feathered joy.
They festoon Earth in vibrant gospel robes.
When April perches on my sill, it sings.

CATEGORY 22 THE CHILDHOOD AWARD

Carolynn J. Scully
Apopka/Forest City, FL

Little Adventures

Little ones rest
in safety of arms
holding the door
open to a land
where bears are friends
with piglets and talk to little boys,
where magic makes toys
come alive and the world is
a place where good always wins.

Little ones listen and dream
of the day they will open the door
and travel through time and space
finding their own quest
for excitement, but until then
they need someone bigger
to show them pictures
read the words
and join them on a trip of a lifetime!

Michele Cuomo
Winter Springs, FL

Islip

I tried to return to you, Islip
your quaint streets
pink Victorian turrets
and the Bay's bracing salt
and the gulls
I thought I had not appreciated you before
remembered again driving the circle
around the town hall with my mother
her leather gloves on the steering wheel
her black bouffant and Jackie O glasses
The Castle Inn so grand that kept changing hands
the big silver dollar sign on a store
the eminence of the bank that once minted bills
the remarkable architecture of St. Marks.
I reveled in you Islip, coming back after a life time
Then, Ian and I took a jog past the veteran's memorial
And the Oconee Inn and the Old Main Street School
It was dusk and you could inhale the sea
I watched Ian's man bun lift up and down
slim legs disappear and reappear exchanging
with the back of his shoes
Then-FAGGOTS!!! We hear from a passing car
Oh yes, I remember now.
That's Islip.
A town so dull hate is a sport

CATEGORY 24 THE ENCHANTMENT AWARD

Cheryl A. Van Beek
Wesley Chapel, FL

Wing Beats

Sometimes when I remember,
to forget my thoughts,
I become the hummingbird moth.

My wings keep time, beat
against Star Gazer Lily's
sticky pistil, read its ruby braille freckles.

I sky dive through time
into its green asterisk center,
bathe in the laving light
of its fuchsia and white
petalled constellation.

I hover, taste the wisdom
of sky and earth in beads
of its raw honey –
sensing
what cannot be spoken.

I breathe time melting –
like steam over clove tea.
My wings beat – rain down on me
a titian pollen storm.

My wings beat – lose time,
scatter it on a Milky way
of lilies glowing in twilight.

Then I forget to forget.
I remember my thoughts,
my feet thud to the ground.
Pollen powders my nose,
wings beat inside me.

CATEGORY 25 THE MIAMI POETS AWARD

Mark Andrew James Terry
Orlando, FL

At a Friend's Grave

I came to you in autumn's fog,
a blushing leaf, a monologue.

Your breeze unhinged my fettered hue.
Detached, I fluttered free. I flew
and floated o'er your flowerbeds.
I noticed shift to downturned heads.

Then, swirl-swam a grieving group
encircling your open grave,
and on your stone the words, God Save,
reminded me to kneel, to stoop

and pray the ones who fell in fall
fulfilled the purpose of their call –
to thrill our hearts, then nourish earth,
becoming part of some new birth.

I thought about the good you did,
the love you had you never hid,
of how you held "we were" of us,
its minus/plus superfluous,

and in dismay I slipped away
to write these words, to try convey
how duly sad I felt that day.

CATEGORY 26 THE EKPHRASTIC POEM AWARD —
Writing Inspired By Art

Mark Andrew James Terry
Orlando, FL

Those I Never Knew
On viewing "Shoes on the Danube Bank,"
a sculpture by Gyula Pauer

I write of those I never knew,
their stories draped in residue
from when the world was blown apart:
gold fillings, bones and stolen art;
of candles in a shoe.

In rusting iron they seem to wait
with others from a kindred state.
As art they're meant to consecrate
that awful queue where bullets flew
through those I never knew.

I saw the shoes in Budapest,
their shadows pointing to protest
where bodies floated, bloated, dressed,
the victims of a grotesque quest
to murder dispossessed.

I wish I had a candle, too,
to light for those I never knew.

Playalinda Beach,
Cheri Neuman Herald

About the Florida State Poets Association

2020-2021 FSPA OFFICERS

Mary Marcelle, President
Mark Andrew James Terry, Vice-President
Sonja Jean Craig, Secretary
Robyn Weinbaum, Treasurer

2020-20201 CERTIFIED FSPA CHAPTERS

Big Bend Poets, Tallahassee
Citrus Poets
Live Poets Society, Daytona Beach
Miami Poets, Pinecrest
New River Poets, Pasco County
North Florida Poetry Hub, Jacksonville
Orlando Area Poets, Maitland
Poetry for the Love of It, Tallahassee
Space Coast Poets, Melbourne
Sunshine Poets, Crystal River
Tomoka Poets, Ormond Beach

FPSA also has many **members at large** who are not affiliated
with a chapter. These members live not only in Florida, but in
various states across the nation and countries around the globe.

NOTE: New members and chapters are welcome. Rules and
requirements are on the FSPA website:
www.floridastatepoetsassociation.org.

FLORIDA STATE POETS ASSOCIATION
History, Objectives, Conferences

The Florida State Poets Association Inc. was founded in 1974 by Henrietta A. Kroah of DeLand, Florida, with the assistance of Han Jurgenson, PhD, of the University of Tampa, a past president of the National Federation of State Poetry Societies (NFSPS). Its main objective is to secure a fuller public recognition of the art of poetry, stimulate a finer and more intelligent appreciation of poetry, and to provide opportunities for the study of poetry and incentives for the writing and reading of poetry. This is accomplished through local member chapters, a quarterly newsletter, and multiple state contests for adults and students. A State Convention is held each October and a spring-time conference is in April.

Visit: www.floridastatepoetsassociation.org
for current events, activities, and member news

* * *

NATIONAL FEDERATION OF
STATE POETRY SOCIETIES

NFSPS is a federation of over thirty state poetry societies. Organized in 1959 and incorporated in 1966, NFSPS provides support to the state member societies through a quarterly newsletter, various national contests, and a convention each June. Over the years FSPA members have been an integral part of the federation.

Visit: www.nfsps.com for further information

Paddleboarding, Daytona Beach
Daniel L. Stone

Made in the USA
Columbia, SC
21 October 2021